THE COMPLETE CAT
ORGANIZER

THE ESSENTIAL PET RECORD KEEPER
AND CAT-CARE HANDBOOK

more help with your pet from

RONNIE
SELLERS
PRODUCTIONS
PORTLAND, MAINE

Published by Ronnie Sellers Productions, Inc.
81 West Commercial Street
Portland, Maine 04101
For ordering information:
(800) 625-3386 toll free
(207) 772-6814 FAX
Visit our Web site: www.rsvp.com • E-mail: rsp@rsvp.com

Publishing Director: Robin Haywood
Managing Editor: Mary Baldwin
Production Artists: Kathy Fisher, Charlotte Smith, Nicole Cyr

ISBN 10: 1-56906-971-9
ISBN 13: 978-1-56906-971-4

Editor: Cricky Long
Design: Carol Salvin
Cover photographs: ©Masterfile/Elizabeth Knox

This book is designed to inform and to entertain. Every effort was made
to ensure that all the information contained in this book was accurate
and up-to-date at the time of publication. However, the author and the
publisher are not veterinarians, and they are in no way responsible
for any loss or damage that may result from any information or errors
contained in this book. **IF YOUR CAT REQUIRES MEDICAL ATTENTION,
CONTACT YOUR VET OR ANIMAL EMERGENCY FACILITY IMMEDIATELY.**

Printed in China

city dog wants to hear from you!

The Complete Cat Organizer is intended for use by everyone who owns a cat. Whether you are prepping your home for a new kitten or just need to add a little organization to your household, this organizer is designed to make your life easier and your cat's life better. We hope you find it to be user-friendly and chock-full of helpful cat information. However, if you find that certain sections could be improved upon, please let us know. We would also love to know which parts of this book you found to be particularly helpful.

To learn more about other City Dog organizational accessories, visit our Web site at citydog. net. Comments, questions, and requests can be made using the form on our Web site at citydog.net or by e-mailing us at editor@citydog.net.

Thank you!

The City Dog Team

BE SURE TO CHECK OUT THESE OTHER GREAT CITY DOG TITLES!

- THE COMPLETE DOG ORGANIZER
- CITY DOG: ATLANTA
- CITY DOG: GREATER BOSTON
- CITY DOG: CHICAGO
- CITY DOG: LOS ANGELES (2ND EDITION)
- CITY DOG: NEW YORK CITY

- CITY DOG: GREATER PHILADELPHIA
- CITY DOG: DALLAS/FORT WORTH
- CITY DOG: SAN FRANCISCO
- CITY DOG: WASHINGTON, D.C.
- CITY DOG: THE NATIONAL HOTEL & RESORT GUIDE

contents

Chapter 3

Chapter 4

Chapter 5

Chapter 1

 CAT VITALS

Record your cat's name, home address, owner information, important care providers, and other cat-related contacts on the forms provided in this section, and all the basic information about your cat that you might want in a hurry will be at your fingertips. Also, this section offers advice on emergency situations and finding help.

in this chapter

- IDENTITY
- DAILY ROUTINE
- OWNER INFORMATION
- HELPFUL PEOPLE
- EMERGENCY CARE
- VETERINARY CARE
- FIRST-AID KIT

- EVACUATION PLAN
- EVACUATION/CAT-FRIENDLY HOTELS
- LOST CAT HELP
- PET-SUPPLY STORES
- PET SITTERS
- BOARDING FACILITIES
- GROOMERS
- CAT BEHAVIORISTS

identity — Cat #1

NAME. . . . .

DATE OF BIRTH . . . .

DATE OF ADOPTION. . . . .

☐ FEMALE   ☐ MALE

BREED(S) . . . .

FUR COLOR(S) . . . .

MARKINGS . . . .

SIZE . . . .

WEIGHT . . . .

MICROCHIP NUMBER . . . .

LOST PET LOCATOR NUMBER (. . . .) . . . .

RABIES VACCINATION
TAG NUMBER . . . .

MEDICATION 1. . . . .

DOSAGE/FREQUENCY . . . .

GIVE WITH . . . .

MEDICATION 2. . . . .

DOSAGE/FREQUENCY . . . .

GIVE WITH . . . .

ALLERGIES . . . .

(Keeping a photo of your cat handy can be important if she becomes lost.)

PICTURE

daily routine — Cat #1

NAME . . . .

EATING

I eat . . . . . ☐ **cup(s)** ☐ **can(s)** of

. . . .

Special preparation . . . .

. . . .

My food is kept . . . .

. . . .

☐ I usually eat breakfast at . . . .

☐ I usually eat dinner at . . . .

☐ I eat once a day at . . . .

☐ I am perfectly capable of managing my own food intake. My bowl should be at least . . . . . full at all times.

☐ I do **not** like to be touched while eating.

My treats are kept . . . .

☐ I am allowed to have . . . . treats a day.

☐ No treats for me — I am

    ☐ on a diet.

    ☐ allergic.

I ☐ **am** ☐ **am not** allowed to eat table scraps.

    ☐ **except** ☐ **only** . . . .

ATTITUDE

Given the opportunity, I will . . .

☐ Curl up in your lap and go to sleep.
☐ Rub against you or look for rubs.
☐ Scratch my scratching post.
☐ Scratch your eyes out.
☐ Escape.
☐ Other.

I may have an issue with

☐ Other cats
☐ Small dogs
☐ Big dogs
☐ All dogs
☐ Visitors
☐ Children
☐ Separation anxiety

identity — Cat #2

NAME . . . .

DATE OF BIRTH . . . .

DATE OF ADOPTION . . . .

☐ FEMALE   ☐ MALE

BREED(S) . . . .

FUR COLOR(S) . . . .

MARKINGS . . . .

SIZE . . . .

WEIGHT . . . .

MICROCHIP NUMBER . . . .

LOST PET LOCATOR NUMBER (. . . .) . . . .

RABIES VACCINATION
TAG NUMBER . . . .

MEDICATION 1 . . . .

DOSAGE/FREQUENCY . . . .

GIVE WITH . . . .

MEDICATION 2 . . . .

DOSAGE/FREQUENCY . . . .

GIVE WITH . . . .

ALLERGIES . . . .

(Keeping a photo of your cat handy can be important if she becomes lost.)

PICTURE

daily routine — Cat #2

NAME. . . . .

EATING

I eat. . . . . ☐ **cup(s)** ☐ **can(s)** of

. . . .

Special preparation . . . .

. . . .

My food is kept . . . .

. . . .

☐ I usually eat breakfast at . . . .

☐ I usually eat dinner at . . . .

☐ I eat once a day at . . . .

☐ I am perfectly capable of managing my own food intake. My bowl should be at least . . . . . full at all times.

☐ I do **not** like to be touched while eating.

My treats are kept . . . .

☐ I am allowed to have . . . . treats a day.

☐ No treats for me — I am

☐ on a diet.

☐ allergic.

I ☐ **am** ☐ **am not** allowed to eat table scraps.

☐ **except** ☐ **only**. . . . .

ATTITUDE

Given the opportunity, I will . . .
☐ Curl up in your lap and go to sleep.
☐ Rub against you or look for rubs.
☐ Scratch my scratching post.
☐ Scratch your eyes out.
☐ Escape.
☐ Other.

I may have an issue with
☐ Other cats
☐ Small dogs
☐ Big dogs
☐ All dogs
☐ Visitors
☐ Children
☐ Separation anxiety

*If you have more than 2 cats, please copy identity & daily routine pages, fill out & keep in tab pocket.

owner information

CAT OWNER 1

Name . . . .

Home phone   (. . . .) . . . . . . ⎯ . . . . . .

Work phone   (. . . .) . . . . . . ⎯ . . . . . .

Cell phone   (. . . .) . . . . . . ⎯ . . . . . .

E-mail . . . .

Other . . . .

Address . . . .

City, state, ZIP . . . .

. . . .

CAT OWNER 2

Name . . . .

Home Phone   (. . . .) . . . . . . ⎯ . . . . . .

Work Phone   (. . . .) . . . . . . ⎯ . . . . . .

Cell Phone   (. . . .) . . . . . . ⎯ . . . . . .

E-mail . . . .

☐ Same address

Address . . . .

City, state, ZIP . . . .

. . . .

Notes . . . .

. . . .

. . . .

. . . .

. . . .

. . . .

. . . .

helpful people

NEIGHBORS, FAMILY MEMBERS, OR CLOSE FRIENDS TO CALL IN AN EMERGENCY

Name . . . .

Home phone　(. . . .)　. . . . . — . . . .

Work phone　(. . . .)　. . . . . — . . . .

Cell phone　(. . . .)　. . . . . — . . . .

E-mail . . . .

Notes . . . .

. . . .

. . . .

. . . .

Name . . . .

Home phone　(. . . .)　. . . . . — . . . .

Work phone　(. . . .)　. . . . . — . . . .

Cell phone　(. . . .)　. . . . . — . . . .

E-mail . . . .

Notes . . . .

. . . .

. . . .

. . . .

Name . . . .

Home phone　(. . . .)　. . . . . — . . . .

Work phone　(. . . .)　. . . . . — . . . .

Cell phone　(. . . .)　. . . . . — . . . .

E-mail . . . .

Notes . . . .

. . . .

. . . .

. . . .

Name . . . .

Home phone　(. . . .)　. . . . . — . . . .

Work phone　(. . . .)　. . . . . — . . . .

Cell phone　(. . . .)　. . . . . — . . . .

E-mail . . . .

Notes . . . .

. . . .

. . . .

. . . .

emergency care

See the critical conditions in **CAT HEALTH (CHAPTER 3)** for information on life-threatening conditions and ailments.

24-HOUR/AFTER-HOURS EMERGENCY FACILITY

☐ Business card in plastic pocket

Facility name . . . .

Phone   (. . . .) . . . . — . . . .

Address . . . .

Closest cross street . . . .

City, state, ZIP . . . .

. . . .

Service hours

Weekdays. . . . . . . — . . . . . . 24/7 ☐

Weekends . . . . . . — . . . . . . 24/7 ☐

Exam Fee $ . . . .

Payment methods
☐ Check   ☐ Credit cards   ☐ Other . . . .

Notes . . . .

. . . .

. . . .

. . . .

ANIMAL AMBULANCE

☐ Business card in plastic pocket

Business Name . . . .

Phone   (. . . .) . . . . — . . . .

Service Hours

Weekdays. . . . . . . — . . . . . . 24/7 ☐

Weekends . . . . . . — . . . . . . 24/7 ☐

Emergency transport fee $ . . . .

Payment methods
☐ Check   ☐ Credit cards   ☐ Other . . . .

Notes . . . .

. . . .

. . . .

. . . .

. . . .

veterinary care

> For information on how to find a good vet, see page 37 in **CAT CONCERNS & CARE.**

PRIMARY VET

☐ Business card in plastic pocket

Facility name . . . .

Veterinarian . . . .

Specialty. . . . .

Phone (. . . .) . . . . — . . . .

E-mail. . . . .

Address . . . .

Closest cross street . . . .

City, state, ZIP. . . . .

Web site . . . .

VET 2

☐ Business card in plastic pocket

Facility name . . . .

Veterinarian . . . .

Specialty. . . . .

Phone (. . . .) . . . . — . . . .

E-mail. . . . .

Address . . . .

Closest cross street . . . .

City, state, ZIP. . . . .

Web site . . . .

Other vets in practice (in order of preference)

1 . . . .

2 . . . .

Office hours

Weekdays. . . . . — . . . .

☐ Closed for lunch

Saturdays. . . . . — . . . .

Sundays. . . . . — . . . .

☐ 24/7

Exam fee $ . . . .

Payment methods
☐ Check ☐ Credit cards ☐ Other . . . .

Other vets in practice (in order of preference)

1 . . . .

2 . . . .

Office hours

Weekdays. . . . . — . . . .

☐ Closed for lunch

Saturdays. . . . . — . . . .

Sundays. . . . . — . . . .

☐ 24/7

Exam fee $ . . . .

Payment methods
☐ Check ☐ Credit cards ☐ Other . . . .

first-aid kit

You should keep a pet first-aid kit on hand for emergencies.

Several companies make comprehensive first-aid kits that you can purchase online. Both Healer Pet Products and Medipet offer a smaller travel kit as well as a more comprehensive home kit.

Healerpetproducts.com
- Home Pet Pak First-aid Kit
- Travel Pet Pak First-aid Kit
- Wallet Pet Pak First-aid Kit

Medipet.com
- Medi+Pet Deluxe First-aid Kit
- Medi+Pet Standard First-aid Kit
- Mini Clip 'N Go Travel First-aid Kit

If you decide to make your own first-aid kit, consider stocking it with the following medications and first-aid supplies. When possible, buy the child's version of the listed medications. Also, buy tablets instead of capsules, because you may have to cut the dosage in half.

MEDICINE CHECKLIST

 TAKE NOTE Always speak to your vet and confirm dosage information before giving human medication to your cat.

☐ Benadryl®

☐ Imodium®

☐ Mineral oil (laxative)

☐ Pedialyte® (for dehydration)

☐ Pepto-Bismol®

> **WARNING!**
> Under no circumstances should you give your cat aspirin, ibuprofen (Advil®, Motrin®), naproxen (Aleve®), or acetaminophen (Tylenol®). These medications are very toxic to your cat.

FIRST-AID SUPPLIES CHECKLIST

☐ Ace bandage

☐ Antibacterial soap

☐ Antibiotic ointment (such as Betadine®)

☐ Antiseptic wipes

☐ Band-Aids®

☐ Blanket (to preserve body heat)

☐ Blunt-edge scissors

☐ Bottled water

☐ Cotton balls

☐ Cotton gauze pad

☐ Cotton gauze roll

☐ Cotton swabs

☐ Disposable cold-compress pack (to alleviate swelling)

☐ Disposable gloves (if there are open wounds)

☐ Disposable hot-compress pack

☐ Eye rinsing solution

☐ Feline thermometer

☐ First-aid tape

☐ Honey packet/sugar (dehydration, shock/hypothermia)

☐ Hot water bottle

☐ Hydrogen peroxide

☐ Liquid bandages (good for paw abrasions)

☐ Matches

☐ Needle and thread

☐ Oral syringes

☐ Petroleum jelly

☐ Rubbing alcohol

☐ Safety pins

☐ Tweezers

☐ Extra doses of your cat's regular medications

evacuation plan

WARNING!

Make sure that anyone you designate to rescue your pets in an emergency has total access to your home. Give this person a set of keys, alarm codes, permission to get past the doorman, etc.

Any one of the following events could force you to evacuate your home with little or no notice:

- Earthquake
- Flood
- Hurricane
- Snowstorm
- Tornado
- Wild fire
- Terrorist attack

A little planning will go a long way toward helping ensure that you and your animals remain safe in an emergency!

- Make a plan with a neighbor, nearby friend, or pet sitter to evacuate your pets in the event that you are unable to get to your house to get them yourself.

- Put together an emergency-evacuation kit for your cat and make sure your emergency backup knows where it is.

- Keep a current list of pet-friendly hotels in surrounding areas. For a listing of hotels, see **CAT-FRIENDLY HOTEL CHAINS** on page 105.

Notes ·

· ·

· ·

· ·

· ·

· ·

EMERGENCY-EVACUATION KIT CHECKLIST

- ☐ Two-week supply of cat food and water
- ☐ One-month supply of medication
- ☐ Cat bed or blanket
- ☐ Two prepackaged disposable litter boxes (be sure to include a scooper)
- ☐ Two bowls
- ☐ Cat carrier labeled with your name and cell phone number (in case you get separated from your cat) as well as the phone number of someone outside the region, in case phone lines go down, cell phone reception towers get wiped out, or the lines get jammed
- ☐ Copy of your cat's vet and vaccination records
- ☐ Copy of your cat's rabies vaccination certificate (make sure to keep it current)
- ☐ Collar with ID tag and/or cell phone number written in permanent marker on collar (nylon)
- ☐ Feeding/medication schedule
- ☐ Portable scratching post or block (flat cardboard-variety blocks found in pet stores are lightweight, space-efficient, and inexpensive
- ☐ Catnip
- ☐ Treats and toys
- ☐ First-aid kit
- ☐ Microchip number . . . .
- ☐ Rabies vaccination number . . . .

With the exception of the cat carrier, store emergency evacuation supplies in an airtight, lightweight bin or trashcan. To prevent items from becoming stale, swap out and use the cat food and water every few months.

EMERGENCY-EVACUATION TIPS

- Do not wait until the last minute to evacuate.
- Do not, under any circumstances, leave your pets behind if you evacuate!
- If you receive a warning (or if you think there is the possibility) that you may need to evacuate, keep your cat confined to an area where you can easily catch her
- Put a collar with an ID tag on your cat, which has your cell phone number as well as the phone number of someone outside the region in case phone lines go down, cell phone reception towers get wiped out, or the lines get jammed
- Secure a reservation at a cat-friendly hotel as soon as possible

Notes . . . .

. . . .

. . . .

. . . .

. . . .

. . . .

. . . .

. . . .

. . . .

. . . .

. . . .

. . . .

evacuation/cat-friendly hotels

HOTEL 1 . . . .

Address . . . .

Closest cross street . . . .

City, state, ZIP . . . .

Phone Number (. . . .) . . . . —

E-mail . . . .

Web site . . . .

Nightly rate

☐ Pet deposit

☐ Pet cleaning fee

☐ Cats are not allowed in the room alone

HOTEL 3 . . . .

Address . . . .

Closest cross street . . . .

City, state, ZIP . . . .

Phone Number (. . . .) . . . . —

E-mail . . . .

Web site . . . .

Nightly rate

☐ Pet deposit

☐ Pet cleaning fee

☐ Cats are not allowed in the room alone

HOTEL 2 . . . .

Address . . . .

Closest cross street . . . .

City, state, ZIP . . . .

Phone Number (. . . .) . . . . —

E-mail . . . .

Web site . . . .

Nightly rate

☐ Pet deposit

☐ Pet cleaning fee

☐ Cats are not allowed in the room alone

HOTEL 4 . . . .

Address . . . .

Closest cross street . . . .

City, state, ZIP . . . .

Phone Number (. . . .) . . . . —

E-mail . . . .

Web site . . . .

Nightly rate

☐ Pet deposit

☐ Pet cleaning fee

☐ Cats are not allowed in the room alone

For information on more accommodations in case of an emergency, see **HELPFUL PEOPLE** *on page 13.*

lost cat help

Having your cat disappear is a very scary thing. Before you send out a search party for your cat, thoroughly check the following places:

FAVORITE CAT HIDING PLACES

- dark and/or partially enclosed spaces
- behind drapes and doors
- behind or underneath dressers, armoires, and other large pieces of furniture
- underneath beds — check inside the box spring if the lining is even a little torn
- on bookshelves — behind books
- in closets — on blankets, clothes, top shelves
- inside cabinets and dresser drawers
- in the dryer
- in the laundry hamper/basket
- inside boxes, suitcases, bags, etc.
- under bed covers
- underneath tablecloths — perched on a chair

Many pieces of large furniture have cavities in the back where cats love to hide. This is especially true of hotel furniture.

Even though it's a hassle, get someone to help you move the furniture if there is even a remote chance that your cat could squeeze into the cavity.

However, you can take some immediate steps that will significantly increase the chances of her safe return.

- Stay calm and make a plan.
- Enlist the help of as many people as you can, and then delegate as many of the tasks on this list as possible.
- Send out a search party. You and anyone else the cat knows and trusts are the best people to search for your cat.
- Call vets and animal hospitals in the area.
- Make and post flyers.
- Check animal shelters at least every other day.
- Consider hiring a pet detective.

> *Cats are not known for their willingness to come when called, and a cat that is disoriented or scared is even less likely to come when called. Bringing along dry food in a plastic bag or empty can (or any other noisemaking treats that tend to draw your cat out) may help entice your cat out of a hiding place.*

FLYER INFORMATION CHECKLIST
- *a color photo of your cat*
- *a list of your cat's stats: approximate size, weight, color, and markings*
- *the offering of a monetary reward for the return of your cat*
- *the statement "needs medication" in big, bold letters (many people believe that a person is more likely to return an animal that needs medication)*

WHERE TO POST FLYERS
- *veterinary clinics*
- *animal emergency facilities*
- *shelters*
- *pet-supply stores*
- *grooming salons*
- *anywhere neighborhood people congregate, such as community centers, coffee shops, bookstores, supermarkets, stores, etc.*

pet-supply stores

Store 1 . . . .

. . . .

☐ Business card in plastic pocket

Phone (. . . .) . . . . — . . . .

Address . . . .

Closest cross street . . . .

City, state , ZIP . . . .

Web site . . . .

Hours

Weekdays . . . . — . . . .

Saturday . . . . — . . . .

Sunday . . . . — . . . .

Payment methods
☐ Check ☐ Credit cards ☐ Other . . . .

Owner/manager(s) . . . .

. . . .

Cat food(s) . . . .

. . . .

Treats/catnip . . . .

. . . .

. . . .

Supplement(s) . . . .

. . . .

. . . .

Flea-prevention treatment . . . .

. . . .

Miscellaneous product(s) . . . .

. . . .

. . . .

. . . .

Foods/products to avoid . . . .

. . . .

Services offered . . . .

. . . .

. . . .

Parking/delivery options . . . .

. . . .

Notes . . . .

. . . .

. . . .

Store 2 . . . .

. . . .

☐ Business card in plastic pocket

Phone   (. . . .) . . . . . — . . . . . .

Address . . . .

Closest cross street . . . .

City, state , ZIP . . . .

Web site . . . .

Hours

   Weekdays . . . . — . . . .

   Saturday . . . . — . . . .

   Sunday . . . . — . . . .

Payment methods
   ☐ Check   ☐ Credit cards   ☐ Other . . . .

Owner/manager(s) . . . .

. . . .

Cat food(s) . . . .

. . . .

Treats/catnip . . . .

. . . .

. . . .

Supplement(s) . . . .

. . . .

. . . .

Flea-prevention treatment . . . .

. . . .

Miscellaneous product(s) . . . .

. . . .

. . . .

. . . .

Foods/products to avoid . . . .

. . . .

Services offered . . . .

. . . .

. . . .

Parking/delivery options . . . .

. . . .

. . . .

Notes . . . .

. . . .

. . . .

pet sitters contact sheet

> See **LOGS & INFO SHEETS (CHAPTER 5)**
> *for Pet Sitter Info Sheets.*

Pet Sitter 1 . . . .

☐ Business card in plastic pocket

Phone (. . . .) . . . . . . — . . . .

Cell/pager (. . . .) . . . . . — . . . .

E-mail . . . .

Web site . . . .

Weekday hours . . . . Rate . . . .

Weekend hours . . . . Rate . . . . . .

Holiday hours . . . . Rate . . . .

Overnight hours . . . . Rate . . . . . .

Pet Sitter 2 . . . .

☐ Business card in plastic pocket

Phone (. . . .) . . . . . . — . . . .

Cell/Pager (. . . .) . . . . . — . . . .

E-mail . . . .

Web site . . . .

Weekdays Hours . . . . Rate . . . .

Weekend Hours . . . . Rate . . . . . .

Holiday Hours . . . . Rate . . . .

Overnights . . . . Rate . . . . . .

Pet Sitter 3 . . . .

☐ Business card in plastic pocket

Phone (. . . .) . . . . . . — . . . .

Cell/Pager (. . . .) . . . . . — . . . .

E-mail . . . .

Web site . . . .

Weekdays Hours . . . . Rate . . . .

Weekend Hours . . . . Rate . . . . . .

Holiday Hours . . . . Rate . . . .

Overnights . . . . Rate . . . . . .

Pet Sitter 4 . . . .

☐ Business card in plastic pocket

Phone (. . . .) . . . . . . — . . . .

Cell/Pager (. . . .) . . . . . — . . . .

E-mail . . . .

Web site . . . .

Weekdays Hours . . . . Rate . . . .

Weekend Hours . . . . Rate . . . . . .

Holiday Hours . . . . Rate . . . .

Overnights . . . . Rate . . . . . .

> *For information on how to find a good pet sitter, see page 47 in* **CAT CONCERNS & CARE.**

boarding facilities

Facility 1 . . . .

☐ Business card in plastic pocket

Phone (. . . .) . . . . . . — . . . .

Address . . . .

Closest cross street . . . .

City, state, ZIP . . . .

E-mail . . . .

Web site . . . .

Office hours

  Weekdays . . . . — . . . .

    ☐ Closed for lunch . . . .

  Saturdays . . . . — . . . .

  Sundays . . . . — . . . .

  ☐ 24/7

Boarding Fee $ . . . .

Payment methods
☐ Check   ☐ Credit cards   ☐ Other . . . .

Facility 2 . . . .

☐ Business card in plastic pocket

Phone (. . . .) . . . . . . — . . . .

Address . . . .

Closest cross street . . . .

City, state, ZIP . . . .

E-mail . . . .

Web site . . . .

Office hours

  Weekdays . . . . — . . . .

    ☐ Closed for lunch . . . .

  Saturdays . . . . — . . . .

  Sundays . . . . — . . . .

  ☐ 24/7

Boarding Fee $ . . . .

Payment methods
☐ Check   ☐ Credit cards   ☐ Other . . . .

For information on how to find a good boarding facility, see page 49 in **CAT CONCERNS & CARE.**

Facility 3 . . . .

☐ Business card in plastic pocket

Phone (. . . .) . . . . . . ⁻ . . . .

Address . . . .

Closest cross street . . . .

City, state, ZIP . . . .

E-mail . . . .

Web site . . . .

Office hours

  Weekdays . . . . ⁻ . . . .

  ☐ Closed for lunch . . . .

  Saturdays . . . . ⁻ . . . .

  Sundays . . . . ⁻ . . . .

  ☐ 24/7

Boarding Fee $ . . . .

Payment methods
  ☐ Check ☐ Credit cards ☐ Other . . . .

Facility 4 . . . .

☐ Business card in plastic pocket

Phone (. . . .) . . . . . . ⁻ . . . .

Address . . . .

Closest cross street . . . .

City, state, ZIP . . . .

E-mail . . . .

Web site . . . .

Office hours

  Weekdays . . . . ⁻ . . . .

  ☐ Closed for lunch . . . .

  Saturdays . . . . ⁻ . . . .

  Sundays . . . . ⁻ . . . .

  ☐ 24/7

Boarding Fee $ . . . .

Payment methods
  ☐ Check ☐ Credit cards ☐ Other . . . .

groomers

Groomer 1	**Groomer 2** . . . .
☐ Business card in plastic pocket	☐ Business card in plastic pocket
Phone (. . . .) . . . . . . —	Phone (. . . .) . . . . . . — . . . .
Address	Address . . . .
Closest cross street	Closest cross street . . . .
City, state, ZIP	City, state, ZIP . . . .
E-mail	E-mail . . . .
Web site	Web site . . . .

Office hours

   Weekdays . . . . — . . . .

    ☐ Closed for lunch . . . .

   Saturdays . . . . — . . . .

   Sundays . . . . — . . . .

   ☐ 24/7

Payment methods
  ☐ Check   ☐ Credit cards   ☐ Other . . . .

Office hours

   Weekdays . . . . — . . . .

    ☐ Closed for lunch . . . .

   Saturdays . . . . — . . . .

   Sundays . . . . — . . . .

   ☐ 24/7

Payment methods
  ☐ Check   ☐ Credit cards   ☐ Other . . . .

For information on how to find a good groomer, see page 45 in **CAT CONCERNS & CARE.**

Groomer 3 . . . .

☐ Business card in plastic pocket

Phone (. . . .) . . . . . . — . . . .

Address . . . .

Closest cross street . . . .

City, state, ZIP . . . .

E-mail . . . .

Web site . . . .

Office hours

  Weekdays . . . . — . . . .

    ☐ Closed for lunch . . . .

  Saturdays . . . . — . . . .

  Sundays . . . . — . . . .

  ☐ 24/7

Payment methods
☐ Check ☐ Credit cards ☐ Other . . . .

Groomer 4 . . . .

☐ Business card in plastic pocket

Phone (. . . .) . . . . . . — . . . .

Address . . . .

Closest cross street . . . .

City, state, ZIP . . . .

E-mail . . . .

Web site . . . .

Office hours

  Weekdays . . . . — . . . .

    ☐ Closed for lunch . . . .

  Saturdays . . . . — . . . .

  Sundays . . . . — . . . .

  ☐ 24/7

Payment methods
☐ Check ☐ Credit cards ☐ Other . . . .

cat behaviorists contact sheet

Behaviorist 1 . . . .

☐ Business card in plastic pocket

Phone (. . . .) . . . . . . ⎺ . . . .

Cell/pager (. . . .) . . . . . . ⎺ . . . .

Address . . . .

Closest cross street . . . .

City, state, ZIP . . . .

E-mail . . . .

Web site . . . .

Hourly rate . . . .

Behaviorist 3 . . . .

☐ Business card in plastic pocket

Phone (. . . .) . . . . . . ⎺ . . . .

Cell/pager (. . . .) . . . . . . ⎺ . . . .

Address . . . .

Closest cross street . . . .

City, state, ZIP . . . .

E-mail . . . .

Web site . . . .

Hourly rate . . . .

Behaviorist 2 . . . .

☐ Business card in plastic pocket

Phone (. . . .) . . . . . . ⎺ . . . .

Cell/pager (. . . .) . . . . . . ⎺ . . . .

Address . . . .

Closest cross street . . . .

City, state, ZIP . . . .

E-mail . . . .

Web site . . . .

Hourly rate . . . .

Behaviorist 4 . . . .

☐ Business card in plastic pocket

Phone (. . . .) . . . . . . ⎺ . . . .

Cell/pager (. . . .) . . . . . . ⎺ . . . .

Address . . . .

Closest cross street . . . .

City, state, ZIP . . . .

E-mail . . . .

Web site . . . .

Hourly rate . . . .

For information on how to find a cat behaviorist, see page 50 in **CAT CONCERNS & CARE.**

Chapter 2

 CAT CONCERNS AND CARE

Owning a cat is a huge commitment, one that will span many years. This section walks you step by step through each phase of ownership: finding the right kitten and preparing your home for her, addressing cat care and behavior issues through the years, and locating support after the loss of a pet.

in this chapter

SO YOU WANT TO GET A KITTEN...

Few things in life are as joyful as getting a kitten. But with a kitten comes a serious long-term commitment — think 20 years — and a great deal of responsibility. In addition to your willingness to care for an animal over a long period of time, think about whether or not your lifestyle will permit you to have a cat. For example, if you move a lot, you may have trouble finding pet-friendly housing; on the other hand, a cat would certainly be a reassuring constant in your life.

Numerous studies have shown that owning a cat brings both emotional and physiological benefits. In addition, cats can be a remarkable source of comfort and companionship for the sick and elderly. Cats, however, do pose certain health risks for persons with compromised immune systems, because they can spread germs, infection, parasites, and disease. (Risks are negligible for people with properly functioning immune systems.) Although there is no way to eliminate these risks altogether, you can minimize them by keeping your cat indoors and not letting strays and/or potentially infectious cats into your home. If you have a compromised immune system, talk to your doctor about the potential risks and benefits of owning a cat before you bring a cat — or any other animal — into your home.

> For more information on cat-related health concerns, see specific topics in the **CAT HEALTH (CHAPTER 3)**.
> - allergies
> - hookworms
> - ringworm
> - roundworms

Compared to a child or even a dog, cats require relatively little care and attention. Some breeds, however, require more care (grooming, exercise, attention, etc.) than others. When deciding whether to get a cat, as well as when choosing a particular breed, consider the following:

- How much time and energy (or money) are you willing to spend grooming your cat?

- How much time and energy are you willing to spend playing with your cat?

- What type of cat will best fit your lifestyle? (For example, if you have, or are planning to start a family, you should look for a breed that is known to be compatible with children.)

For information about various cat breeds, breed-specific traits, and breeder information, check out the Cat Fanciers Web site, www.fanciers.com.

> **KITTEN CARE RESPONSIBILITIES**
> - vaccinations
> - litter box training
> - spaying/neutering
> - kitten proofing your home
>
> **LIFELONG CAT CARE RESPONSIBILITIES**
> - grooming
> - feeding
> - litter box cleaning
> - exercise
> - veterinary care
> - arranging for daily care when you travel

A WILL FOR YOUR PET?

Don't forget about your cat when you write your will. If you don't make arrangements for your cat, she could wind up in a shelter and be euthanized within days.

Be sure to have an attorney confirm that everything has been properly documented and address the following:

- Who will become your cat's guardian if she outlives you
- How much money you are leaving for your cat's care, and how that money should be spent
- Where your cat's medical records are kept

LEGAL AID

We live in an increasingly litigious world, and there are myriad reasons why you might need a pet attorney to represent you, including:

- Estate planning for your pet(s)
- Disputes with landlords or neighbors
- Veterinary malpractice
- Your cat being attacked by, or attacking, another animal
- Disputes with animal control

The Animal Legal Defense Fund provides a list of lawyers (sorted by state) who practice animal law exclusively. For more information, check out the Web site at www.aldf.org.

PET INSURANCE

Pet insurance serves as a safeguard against expensive medical bills resulting from unforeseeable conditions such as cancer, broken bones, and emergency surgical procedures.

Most policies require you to pay a monthly premium, which can range from $15 to $70, as well as a $50 deductible for each visit to the vet or emergency room. For an additional cost, you can also purchase an add-on plan, which provides an allowance for routine visits such as annual exams, vaccinations, and teeth cleanings. If you want to purchase pet insurance, consider doing so while your cat is a kitten — before she has time to develop any "preexisting conditions."

The good news is that pet insurance plans allow you to choose any licensed veterinarian you like. However, you must pay your entire bill up-front and file a claim for reimbursement. There are no family plans, but most companies offer discounts when you sign up multiple pets (usually about 10 percent off each additional plan).

NATIONAL PET INSURANCE COMPANIES

- VPI Pet Insurance (petinsurance.com)
- PetCare (petcareinsurance.com)

5 WORST TIMES TO GET A KITTEN

1. When you start a new job
2. When you know you'll be traveling
3. When you are planning to move
4. When you or your spouse is pregnant
5. During a holiday season

finding the right kitten

- If you are going to buy a purebred kitten, take the time to find a reputable breeder who can show you papers on the kitten's parents.

- Spend the extra money to buy a kitten from a conscientious breeder. Otherwise, you will almost certainly wind up paying at least twice as much later in vet bills.

> ### PICKING THE RIGHT BREEDER
> *Generally, the amount of time and effort a breeder invests in evaluating you, as a potential cat owner, is directly proportional to the quality of that breeder's litters.*
> - Trust your instincts — if something doesn't feel right, it most likely isn't (for example, you should be very concerned if a breeder refuses to show you where he or she keeps the litters).
> - Meet the kitten's parents.
> - In addition to passing on her genes, a mother greatly affects her young's behavior and personality in later life through her temperament and ability to care for, teach, and interact with them.
> - While male cats have no part in raising kittens, it is widely believed that male cats pass on not just physical attributes but also personality traits to their offspring.
> - Do not buy a kitten on impulse.
> - Do not buy a kitten as a gift for someone else unless you are ready, willing, and able to assume responsibility and care for the kitten.

- Make sure the breeder keeps litters inside the family home, to help ensure that kittens receive plenty of human interaction during the early, formative weeks of their lives. Early human interaction has a huge impact on an adult cat's behavior and willingness to interact with people.

ADOPTING A KITTEN VERSUS BUYING A KITTEN

Pet-supply stores that hold adoptions in their stores are in no way affiliated with the kitten mill industry, and the pet stores do not profit from the adoption of the kittens and cats. In fact, animals available at adoption events at pet-supply stores are almost exclusively animals that have been rescued from shelters or abandoned by their owners. And adoption fees are used to offset the cost of the supplies and care of the animals.

> ### WHATEVER YOU DO, DO NOT BUY A KITTEN FROM A PET STORE!
> *Most kittens sold in pet stores come from kitten mills, which mass-produce cats with no regard for the importance of carefully pairing mates to produce genetically sound litters. As a result, kittens from pet stores are much more likely to have breed-specific health issues than are cats bred by reputable, conscientious breeders. Furthermore, the conditions in kitten mills are atrocious. Neither the mother nor the kittens receive adequate care, veterinary or otherwise, which also affects the lifelong health of the kittens. Many people think that by buying kittens from a pet store, they are rescuing them. While that may be true, they are also perpetuating this detestable industry. As long as people continue to buy animals from pet stores, pet stores will keep kitten mills in business by continuing to purchase their kittens.*

kitten proofing your home

- Tuck all cords away or purchase cord covers to prevent your kitten from gnawing on electrical cords.

- Place all plants out of reach — kittens will attempt to eat and climb them.

- Make sure all cabinets, pantries, and closets containing cleaners, toxic chemicals, medicines, etc., can be securely closed. If necessary, install child-safety locks.

- Put away all fragile items.

- Close doors to rooms that are off limits.

- Keep counters and table free of food and anything else that might entice your kitten to jump up.

- Keep bathroom doors closed to prevent your kitten from:
  - Shredding toilet paper
  - Falling into the toilet and drowning
  - Getting into makeup, toiletries, soap, and perfumes
- Make sure windows are escape proof.
- Do not leave the dryer door open. Always check to make sure your cat hasn't slipped into the dryer before starting it.
- Do not leave cords for shades or draperies dangling; your cat can get tangled up in them and strangle herself.
- Do not toss food, especially chicken and turkey bones, into any trashcan that your cat can get into.
- Do not leave your cat in a room unattended with a burning candle.

Notes . . . .

. . . .

. . . .

. . . .

. . . .

. . . .

. . . .

litter box training

For many cats, litter box training requires nothing more than showing them where the litter box is located. However, there are definite measures you can take to make the box as appealing as possible to your cat.

TRAINING YOUR CAT TO USE A LITTER BOX

- Place the box in a quiet area.
- Make sure your cat has easy access to the box 24 hours a day.
- Make sure the sides of the box are low enough that your cat can easily enter and exit.
- Make sure the box is big enough that your cat can comfortably stand, scrape, and turn around in it.
- Clean the box daily and change the litter at least once a week, more frequently for multiple-cat households.
- Make sure you have at least one litter box per cat. Many vets recommend adding one additional box, in case any of the cats should develop an aversion to their box.

LITTER BOX HYGIENE

- Scoop the litter box at least once a day.
- Change the litter at least once a week.
- Clean the box using hot, soapy water. Do not use astringent chemical cleaners, scented soap, ammonia, or vinegar. If you use bleach, be sure to dilute it well (at least nine parts water for every one part bleach) and make sure to rinse the box thoroughly.
- Mix unscented baking soda into the litter to alleviate odors.

Always wash your hands with hot, soapy water after cleaning the box and/or changing the litter. In addition to thoroughly washing your hands after coming into contact with your cat's litter box, you may also want to wear disposable plastic gloves.

> **KEEPING DOGS OUT OF THE LITTER BOX**
> *Disgusting as we may find it, many dogs consider cat feces a particularly tasty treat. The simplest way to prevent your dog from dining out of the litter box is to block his access to it. Provided your cat has no problem jumping over it, a baby gate works well. There are also pills you can put in your cat's food that will make her waste less appealing, but these pills are not 100 percent effective in deterring dogs.*

soiling outside the litter box

If you discover that your cat is eliminating outside her litter box, the first thing you should do is take her to the vet to find out if there is a medical explanation for this behavior. (For example, if your cat is getting old, she may be having a hard time getting in and/or out of the box.) If your cat gets a clean bill of health from your vet, then you need to look into other reasons your cat may be avoiding the litter box.

COMMON REASONS A CAT STOPS USING THE LITTER BOX

- It's dirty.

- It stinks. (The offensive odor may be from perfumed litter and deodorizers, which many cats find equally if not more offensive than their waste.)

- It does not feel safe. (For example, if the dog terrorizes the cat every time she uses the litter box, she's not going to feel particularly secure about using it.)

- The texture of the litter is unacceptable.

- There is too much/not enough litter in the box.

- There is a liner in the box.

- It's too close to her food, water, and/or bed.

QUICK FIXES FOR LITTER BOX AVERSIONS

- Clean the litter box.
- Change the location of the litter box.
- Change the type of litter.
- Remove the litter box cover.

TIPS FOR GETTING YOUR CAT TO STOP SOILING OUTSIDE THE BOX

- Thoroughly clean all areas your cat has soiled, neutralizing all odors.
- Once the area has been cleaned, play with and/or feed your cat in the area so that she associates it with feeding rather than eliminating.
- If your cat continues to soil in the area, place a litter box there to get her back into the habit of using the litter box, then gradually move the box to a more desirable location.
- When all else fails, block your cat's access to the area until she has been retrained to use the box.

Notes . . . .

. . . .

. . . .

. . . .

shopping list

ESSENTIALS FOR YOUR NEW CAT

- **COLLAR AND TAG** Even if you plan to keep your cat indoors, it is a good idea for her to wear a collar and ID tag in case someone accidentally lets her outside. You may also want to consider having a microchip implanted in your cat.

- **CAT CARRIER** Pet stores sell kennel-type carriers as well as inexpensive cardboard boxes. The latter is fine if all you're using it for is trips to the vet and/or groomer.

- **BOWLS** You'll need two bowls, one for food and one for water. Stainless steel bowls are easy to clean and indestructible, and they come in many varieties, including "no-tip" styles.

- **KITTY TREATS** Pet stores have plenty to choose from. Look for a healthier brand that's also good for your cat's teeth.

- **CATNIP** No cat should be deprived of catnip. It's particularly handy in teaching cats to use scratching posts and/or their toys.

- **KITTEN FOOD** Ask your veterinarian or the pet supply store manager to recommend a good brand for your kitten. (The healthier cat foods are available only through pet-supply stores and veterinary offices, not grocery stores.)

- **GROOMING BRUSH** It's a good idea to get your kitten used to being brushed and handled while she is still a kitten. How much you work on this depends largely on how much maintenance the cat will require as an adult.

- **CAT SHAMPOO** Kittens are notorious for getting into things and making messes, so have some gentle cat-approved shampoo on hand. (Many shampoos that are approved for use on dogs are not safe to use on cats, so always read the label first.)

- **CLAW CLIPPERS** If you get your kitten used to having her claws clipped when she is small, claw clipping will be much less of an issue as she gets older. (See **CLAW TRIMMING** on page 53 for more information.)

- **TOYS** Kittens need toys to play with, and pet stores sell tons of them, in all shapes and sizes. Buy a variety until you see what your cat likes. **WARNING!** Make sure toys are not potential choking hazards. **Do not** leave toys with string (or plain string) lying around because your cat could easily choke. Use these types of toys only under supervision.

- **BEDDING** Cats tend to prefer things that are fuzzy or furry. You don't need to buy anything fancy; just make sure it's machine washable.

- **TOOTHBRUSH AND TOOTHPASTE** It's important to get your cat used to having you handle her mouth and brushing her teeth as early as possible. (See **DENTAL HYGIENE** on page 58 for more information.)

- **BITTER APPLE SPRAY** Spray bitter apple on anything you don't want your cat to chew, including furniture, electric and phone cords, and bandages.

- **LITTER** There are many kinds of litter. At some point, most cats will develop a preference for one kind over another. Most cats do not like perfumed litter.

- **LITTER BOX** Depending on the size of your kitten, you may need to start with a smaller box that has lower sides and trade it for a bigger one as your kitten grows.

- **LITTER BOX SCOOP**

- **SCRATCHING POST**

- **HARNESS AND LEASH**

how to find a vet

One of the very first things you will need to do when you get a kitten or cat is to find a vet. In fact, many breeders, rescue groups, and shelters now insist that potential owners find a vet before they are permitted to take a kitten home. The best way to find a good vet is to survey in-the-know cat-o-philes — friends, neighbors, cat rescuers, groomers, pet sitters, day-care owners, cat behaviorists, and owners or managers of pet-supply stores. When you start to hear the same name over and over again, you have probably found a vet worth considering.

QUESTIONS TO ASK CAT-O-PHILES IN YOUR VET QUEST

- In what context do you know the vet? (Is your cat a patient or do you know the vet personally?)
- How difficult is it to get an appointment?
- Can the office accommodate last-minute appointments and emergencies?
- What is the vet's bedside manner like?
- How does the support staff treat you and your cat?
- What do you like best and least about the vet or practice?

While you'll never be certain you've found the right vet until you meet her or him, you can certainly do a preliminary screening by calling the vet's office and speaking to the support staff.

QUESTIONS TO ASK A POTENTIAL VETERINARY CLINIC OR OFFICE

- What is the cost of a routine exam?
- What are the vet's credentials?
- How many years of experience does the vet have?
- How many years has the practice been in business?
- Will your cat see the same vet each time or be relegated to whoever is available on a particular day?
- Are there any specialists (cardiologists, oncologists, orthopedic surgeons, etc.) on staff?
- Does the practice offer any alternative treatment options, such as acupuncture, chiropractic, or herbal therapies?
- What 24-hour or after-hours emergency facility does the vet refer patients to?

> *Once you have found a vet you like, enter his or her info in* **VETERINARY CARE** **(CHAPTER 1).**

bringing a new kitten home

If you already have cats, do not bring home a new cat until your vet has checked her out and vaccinated her. Otherwise, you run the risk of exposing your cat(s) to numerous life-threatening diseases, as well as parasites. People and other pets are also susceptible to parasitic infections, such as ringworm and roundworms, so this is a good policy even if you don't have other cats at home.

Once your vet has given the new kitten a clean bill of health, take the time to kitten proof your home and create a secure space for your kitten. Even the most easy-going, confident kitten/cat will need to adjust to a new person and a new home. To make the transition a little smoother for your cat, consider confining her to one room or area of the house for a few days while she becomes acclimated to the new environment. (This will also buy you time to kitten proof the rest of your house.) Keeping the cat in a single area is especially important if you already have a cat and/or other animals in your home — it will give them time to get used to the new kitten.

introducing a new kitten to your cats

TIPS FOR INTRODUCING A NEW KITTEN TO YOUR OTHER CATS

- Keep the new kitten in a separate room, or a separate area of the house, for the first several days.

- Rub a cloth over each animal, then place it by the other cat, underneath a treat, so both cats learn to positively associate the scent of the other cats with treats.

- After several days, open doors so that the cats can enter each other's space — but make sure each cat has an escape route and safe space that she can retreat to.

- If the cats fight, separate them as quickly as possible (without risking injury to yourself) and keep them separated for at least 24 hours.

- Play with your cats when they're together so that they learn to associate each other with playtime, attention, and toys.

- Do not expect the cats to share. Each cat in your household should have her own food dishes, litter box, scratching post, etc.

Notes

vaccinations

FVRCP

This three-in-one shot series immunizes cats against:

- Feline rhinotracheites
- Feline calcivirus (FCV)
- Feline panleukopenia virus (FPV), also known as feline distemper

Kittens under 16 weeks require three doses of this vaccine:

- Between six and eight weeks of age
- Between nine and 11 weeks
- Between 12 and 16 weeks

Kittens 16 weeks or older require only one dose. The vaccine should be followed up with a booster at one year, followed by subsequent boosters every three years.

Rabies

You are legally required to have your cat (indoor or outdoor) vaccinated against rabies. The first vaccination is good for one year, with subsequent booster vaccinations required at one- or three-year intervals.

Kittens should be vaccinated at 12 weeks.

It used to be universally recommended that cats be given booster shots every year. Now, however, there is some concern that vacci-nating cats too frequently can lead to serious health problems, including vaccine-associated feline sarcoma. The general consensus is that you should give your cat a booster shot at one year of age, with subsequent boosters given every three years. Be sure to speak to your vet before altering your cat's schedule for booster shots.

 You can wait three years only if a three-year (as opposed to annual) vaccine is used. There are no laws that require you to have your animal vaccinated against rabies annually.

ALWAYS KEEP RABIES VACCINATION CURRENT!

Authorities recommend immediate euthanization when a wild animal bites an unvaccinated domestic animal. Cats that have been vaccinated are usually quarantined for 10 days, non-vaccinated cats are quarantined for up to six months, if owners refuse to euthanize them.

Although movies and books often depict rabid dogs, recently there have been more reported cases of cats with rabies than any other animal. Because rabies is so easily transmittable and deadly, it is recommended that indoor cats, which could conceivably get out accidentally, also be vaccinated against rabies.

NON-CORE VACCINATIONS

Additional vaccinations are available for several serious diseases. However, they are not without side effects, they are not 100 percent effective, and they are not usually necessary for indoor cats. If your cat has access to the outdoors or is exposed to potentially infected cats, talk to your vet about whether she is a good candidate for these vaccinations.

FeLV (Feline Leukemia Virus)

First dose   Eight weeks
Second dose   12 weeks (or a minimum of three to four weeks after the first dose)

This vaccine should be followed up with a booster at one year, then annually thereafter.

FIPV (Feline Infectious Peritonitis)

First dose   16 weeks
Second dose   20 weeks (or a minimum of three to four weeks after the first dose)

This vaccine should be followed up with a booster at one year, then annually thereafter.

Chlamydia

Live Vaccine
First dose   Between six and 12 weeks

Killed Vaccine
First dose   Six to nine weeks
Second dose   Nine to 12 weeks (or a minimum of three to four weeks after the first dose)

This vaccine should be followed up with a booster at one year, then annually thereafter.

Notes

· ·

· ·

· ·

· ·

· ·

· ·

· ·

· ·

· ·

spaying/neutering

People have a variety of reasons for **not** wanting to sterilize their cats, but it is in the best interest of your cat, and the animal population as a whole, to do so. Both spaying and neutering are routine surgeries that can be performed in most veterinary offices. (Females are spayed by removing their reproductive organs; males are neutered by removing their testicles.) If the cost of the surgery is an issue, check with local animal-rescue groups to see if they have any spay/neuter discount coupons or know of any low-cost spay/neuter clinics. Some organizations now have mobile spay/neuter clinics to make it even more convenient for pet owners to get their animals sterilized.

Notes

TOP REASONS TO SPAY OR NEUTER YOUR CAT

Neutering or spaying does not make your cat fat. However, an altered cat requires approximately 25 percent fewer calories than an unaltered cat. If you don't adjust your cat's diet accordingly, your cat will gain weight. This is not a good reason not to spay or neuter your cat. The health risks of not altering your animal far outweigh any benefits.

- Sterilizing pets helps control the animal population.

- Spayed/neutered animals live up to three years longer than their unaltered counterparts.

- Spaying your pet before her first estrus, or heat, cycle greatly reduces her chances of getting breast cancer and eliminates the possibility of uterine and ovarian cancers.

- Neutered males are less aggressive or territorial than non-neutered males and therefore sustain fewer injuries.

- Neutered males are less likely to "mark their territory" by spraying.

- Neutered males are less likely to roam/run away than unaltered males.

Each year 8 million animals are euthanized because they do not have homes. By spaying or neutering your cat, you are doing your part to help curb the pet overpopulation crisis.

INDOORS VERSUS OUTDOORS
the advantages of keeping your cat indoors

There are numerous arguments for allowing a cat to go outdoors. But no matter how valid those arguments may be, the reality is that cats with access to the outdoors have a much shorter lifespan (three to five years) than indoor cats, whose lifespan often extends into their late teens or twenties.

INDOOR CATS ARE PROTECTED FROM:
- Abuse, torment, or torture by kids (or adults)

- Being bitten or killed by another animal

- Hit by a car

- Lost

- Stolen

- Picked up by animal control

- Exposed to infectious diseases

- Being poisoned by toxins in the environment (neighbors' trash, fertilizer, insecticide, toads, antifreeze, etc.)

- Sunburn

HOW TO MAKE AN OUTDOORS CAT HAPPY INDOORS
- Provide your cat with plenty of active playtime.

- When you go out, leave lots of little toys around the house for your cat to find. Cats love furry catnip-laden mice (available at pet-supply stores); even balled up socks can keep them entertained.

- Invest in a scratching post, or a multi-level "kitty condo." It may not be what you had in mind when you decorated your home, but it just might keep your cat from destroying your furniture. (For more information see **SCRATCHING** on page 52.)

- Consider adopting another cat or kitten to keep your cat company.

- Get some cat grass for your kitty to munch on (available in most pet-supply stores).

- Create a sunny perch for your cat by a window or glass door.

- Make sure your cat knows where the litter box is.

> You'll never break your cat of her natural instincts. And there is no question that bringing a contented outdoors cat indoors will require a short period of adjustment. But with a little effort, you can redirect her behavior so that she can enjoy her innate activities while remaining safely inside without destroying your home.

HOW TO PROTECT YOUR HOUSE
- If your cat eats or chews on your plants, use Bitter Apple spray on them.

- If your cat digs in the dirt in your plant pots, either put them out of reach or cover the soil with pebbles or marbles.

- Use two-sided tape or other deterrents on any furniture or décor your cat scratches.

- For more tips, see **KITTEN PROOFING YOUR HOME** on page 33.

- If you run into a real problem, hire a cat behaviorist to address the problem before it gets out of control.

walking your cat

One way to keep an indoors-only cat entertained and exposed to the outside is to teach her to walk with a harness. In case you haven't already figured this out, however, cats are not quite as compliant as dogs, and teaching them to wear a harness, let alone walk on a leash, can be a real challenge. But with patience — and a relatively cooperative cat — it is often (but not always) doable.

Unquestionably, the best time to get a cat comfortable wearing a harness and being on a leash is while she is still a kitten.

BUY A HARNESS AND LEASH

You should be able to find a cat harness (one that goes around the neck and the front legs) and leash at most of the larger pet-supply stores. Many stores offer adjustable pet harnesses so you can spare your cat the trip to the pet store to try it on for size.

GETTING YOUR CAT COMFORTABLE WITH THE HARNESS

Take your time getting your cat used to the harness. Try leaving it out by the food bowl, so your cat will associate it with something positive. At some point, you should be able to slip the harness on. Once you've accomplished this, and rewarded her with healthy treats, give your cat time to get used to wearing the harness around the house.

GETTING YOUR CAT COMFORTABLE WITH THE LEASH

Next, you will want to attach the leash. (Again, shower her with treats while you are putting the leash on.) Let her wander freely (under supervision) with the leash attached so that she get comfortable with it. At some point, pick up the leash and follow your cat around the house, so she gets used to the idea of being connected to you. (Again, dispensing treats all the while should help.)

TAKING YOUR CAT FOR A WALK

If you and your cat have made it this far, you are most likely ready to venture outside for a short walk. Be sure to hold onto the leash at all times. Your cat will be on sensory overload, especially if she has never been outside, and you definitely do not want to give her the opportunity to take off if she gets startled. You should also be on the lookout for, and protect your cat from, dogs and other creatures that may attempt to attack or scare your cat. If you need to pick up your cat, be very careful.

 If your cat is scared or excited (which is more than likely on the first several walks), she may attempt to scratch or bite you.

> Do not lose your cool. Yelling at or in any way punishing your cat is counterproductive. Despite your best efforts, your cat may not tolerate wearing a harness or being constrained by a leash. Remember, you are doing this to provide your cat with stimulation and entertainment, not to prove that you can train your cat to walk on a leash. If your efforts are causing your cat distress, stop. You can always try again later. If your cat does not come around after repeated attempts, it may be time to find other sources of excitement for her.

seasonal concerns/tips for outdoor cats

If you are unable to keep your cat indoors all the time, you should take the following precautions. Although taking these steps will reduce the risk of your cat's exposure to harm, they are in no way a guarantee of her safety.

COLD-WEATHER TO DO LIST

- Increase your cat's food

- Make sure your cat has access to shelter and a warm, dry bed. Even the garage is better than nothing

COLD-WEATHER HAZARDS

- Toxins:
  - Antifreeze
  - De-icing salt
  - Holiday foods
- Frostbite
- Hypothermia
- Regional . . . .

. . . .

- Other . . . .

. . . .

. . . .

. . . .

If you think your cat might have come in contact with de-icing salt, be sure to wipe down her paws and stomach with a wet cloth. This will prevent her from ingesting toxins. Also, pay attention to any leaks under your car. The same deadly toxin found in antifreeze is also in radiator coolant. If your car is leaking, be sure to get it checked as soon as possible and make sure your cat does not have access to the spillage.

WARM-WEATHER TO DO LIST

- Buy sunscreen for light-coated cats.
- Start flea and tick treatment.
- Keep your cat indoors during the heat of the day.

WARM-WEATHER HAZARDS

- Fleabites and tick bites
- Heartworm disease
- Heat stroke
- Lyme disease
- Regional . . . .

. . . .

- Other . . . .

. . . .

See **LOGS & INFO SHEETS (CHAPTER 5)** *for Vet Info Sheets.*

See specific listings in **CAT HEALTH (CHAPTER 3)** *for treatment information on the above hazards.*

CAT CARE PROVIDERS
groomer

Depending on the length of your cat's coat and your cat's overall hygiene, you may need to find a good groomer. By relegating your cat-washing duties to a professional, you also get to skip the following hygienic procedures, which usually come standard with full-service grooming: claw trimming, ear cleaning, and anal-gland expression. Many grooming salons also offer optional amenities such as anesthesia-free teeth cleaning and spa services such as cat massage and aromatherapy.

QUESTIONS TO ASK A GROOMER AND THINGS TO CONSIDER

- How long has the salon been in business?
- What is the general atmosphere?:
  - How do the groomers and staff treat the animals?
  - Are the cats and dogs kept in separate areas? (This decreases a cat's stress level.)
  - Are animals groomed assembly-line-style, or do groomers provide personalized service?
  - How clean is the salon?
  - How much experience does the groomer have with cats?
  - Is the groomer certified as a master groomer?

 A certified master groomer is a groomer who has undergone extensive training to groom dogs per the breed standard. The advantage of going with a certified master groomer is that even though their training has been on dogs, they still have had the most training.

- What methods does the groomer use — hand scissoring or clipping?

 Hand scissoring requires more skill and takes longer, but the end result is much more polished.

- How are the cats dried? By hand? By a cage dryer? By a fan?

TAKE NOTE When used improperly, a heated cage dryer can cause heat stroke and kill a cat in a matter of minutes. If your groomer uses cage dryers, make sure the dryers are temperature-controlled and that cats are supervised at all times during the drying process.

- What types of shampoos are used? (Dog and "people" shampoos, as well as dish-washing soaps and detergents, are not pH-balanced for cats.)

- Does the salon offer medicated and/or hypoallergenic shampoos for cats with fleas, itchy skin, or hot spots?

- What are the drop-off and pickup hours?

- How far in advance do you need to schedule an appointment?

ANAL-GLAND EXPRESSION

Fluid builds up inside a cat's anal glands. Typically, this fluid is clear and is released when a cat defecates. As cats age, however, the fluid becomes darker and thicker, which causes it to get stuck. In these instances, the anal glands need to be expressed by a vet or trained groomer.

CLAW TRIMMING

Trimming a cat's claws means snipping off the very end, the dead part of the claw, in the same way that you clip your fingernails. While many cats find the process incredibly aggravating, it is not painful and does not cause any damage to the claw. Many cat owners ask their groomer or vet tech to trim their cat's claws (which is not the same as declawing). (See page 53 for instructions on how to trim your cat's claws yourself.)

EAR CLEANING

Unless there is an underlying infection, which would require a trip to the vet, cats' ears do not require cleaning. However, if the groomer gets water in the ear, he or she will usually administer an antibacterial rinse to prevent infection.

TREATING MATTED FUR

If your cat's hair is badly matted, a groomer or vet will often shave the cat's entire body. (For information on how you can address matted fur at home, see page 61 in this section.)

SEASONAL CLIP

Some cat owners get their cat a lion's cut or completely shave their cat in the summer. Be sure to tell the groomer to leave enough hair to protect your cat from sunburn. It is important to note that cats' hair actually insulates them from the heat, so a clipped cat is likely to be just as hot as, and possibly even hotter than, an unclipped cat.

MOBILE GROOMING

As mobile grooming becomes more popular, grooming vans are becoming increasingly high-tech. They also tend to be cleaner than salons because of the lower traffic volume. Beyond the obvious perk of having your cat groomed in your driveway — so neither you nor your cat has to endure the car trip to the groomer — mobile grooming offers other advantages:

- Your cat gets more personal attention.
- Your cat doesn't have to spend time cooped up in a crate or cage. This is particularly an advantage for older cats, who tend to get stiff or sore when confined.
- You have the convenience of not having to drop off or pick up your cat.

TAKE NOTE Many groomers require electricity and water hookups, so unless you can supply them with access to both, check first to make sure they are self-contained. You pay for the convenience of having a groomer come to you. While most mobile groomers do not charge a travel fee, the cost is generally reflected in the grooming bill.

> For more information on hygienic procedures you can perform at home, see **MORE ON GROOMING** on page 60 in this section.

pet sitter

Cats not only deserve but need daily care. This does not mean you should never leave your house again! If you do go out of town, however, you need to arrange for someone (a pet sitter, neighbor, or friend) to check on your cat daily. At the very least, someone should stop by every 24 hours to feed your cat, change the water, scoop the litter box, and make sure everything is all right. In a perfect world, that person would also spend at least 15 to 20 minutes petting, grooming, playing, and/or just sitting with your cat.

If you decide to hire a professional pet sitter, you have many options. Pet-sitting companies are popping up all over the country. The first thing to decide is whether to go with a big-business pet-sitting company or with an individual. One is not necessarily better than the other; it really comes down to your personal preference.

INDIVIDUAL PET SITTER

PROS

- Your cat gets the same sitter each visit.
- It feels more personal than a pet-sitting company.
- You know who has the key to your home.

CONS

- Unless your sitter has a committed backup, there is no one to fill in if he or she has an emergency and can't make it.
- You are relying on one person's availability.

QUESTIONS TO ASK

- Is pet sitting this person's full-time or part-time job? (A part-time sitter often has a harder time accommodating your schedule and/or last-minute requests.)
- How long has this person been working as a pet sitter?
- Does this person have any formal animal-care training?

BIG-BUSINESS PET-SITTING COMPANY

PROS

- Someone will be able to fill in if your regular pet sitter suddenly can't make it.
- The company screens employees for you, and some even do background checks.
- Employees are usually required to attend some sort of training program or session.

CONS

- You and your pet don't develop a connection with an individual sitter.
- Your cat may not get the same sitter each visit.
- "Company policy" can translate into more surcharges and less flexibility.

QUESTIONS TO ASK

- What sort of screening process does the company use when hiring employees?
- How does the company train its employees?
- How long has the company been in business?
- Will the same pet sitter visit your cat each time?

THE PET SITTER CONSULTATION

It's a good idea to consult with the pet sitter before hiring him or her to spend time alone with your cat. This initial meet-and-greet gives you the opportunity to ask the pet sitter questions while he or she assesses your needs and meets your cat.

QUESTIONS TO ASK A POTENTIAL SITTER

- Is the sitter a member of Pet Sitters International (PSI) or a similar organization?

- Is the sitter bonded and insured?

- Is the sitter certified in pet first-aid and CPR?
- Does the sitter work evenings/weekends/holidays?
- Can the sitter accommodate last-minute appointments?
- Does the sitter do any other household chores (e.g., closing/opening blinds, taking out the trash, feeding other animals, cleaning the litter box, collecting the mail)?
- Will the sitter spend the night at your house? If yes, what time does he or she arrive and leave?
- If necessary, will the sitter administer medication?

- Has the sitter ever had to deal with an emergency while pet sitting? If yes, how did he or she resolve the situation?
- What procedures does he or she have in place for emergencies?
- What vet and/or emergency facility would the sitter use in the event of an emergency?
- Does the sitter offer discount packages?
- Does the sitter charge premiums for any services?
- Will the sitter supply you with references? (Always check references!)

Most pet sitters will administer medications in pill form. If your cat requires injections or more involved care, consider hiring a sitter who has been trained as a vet tech. Many working vet techs moonlight as pet sitters.

Your pet sitter should provide you with a list of rates and fees as well as a pet-sitting contract.

See **LOGS & INFO SHEETS (CHAPTER 5)** *for Pet Sitter Info Sheets.*

---

 5 **SUREFIRE WAYS TO DRIVE YOUR PET SITTER CRAZY**

1. Leave the house alarm on without providing the code. Or even better, give your pet sitter the code, then change it without telling him or her.

2. Wait until the last possible moment to cancel the visit.

3. Hide food, treats, toys, and litter scooper.

4. Never pay on time.

5. Leave lots of illegible notes.

boarding facility

If hiring a pet sitter is not a viable option for you, you can always take your cat to a boarding facility when you go away. In addition to stand-alone boarding facilities, many veterinary offices and some groomers also offer boarding.

At the very least, you should interview a boarding facility over the phone before sending your cat there. However, you should also stop by in advance — not when you're rushing to catch a plane — and ask for a tour so you can decide whether you feel comfortable leaving your cat there.

QUESTIONS TO ASK

- What sort of training has the staff had?

- Is someone on the premises 24 hours a day?

- Is there a vet on call in the event of an emergency, or if your cat gets sick?

- How often do the cats get taken out of their cages? For how long?

- What type of food does the facility provide? Can you bring your own food for your cat?

- What are the facility's feeding policies? Are cats allowed to eat at will, or are there set feeding times?

- If necessary, will the facility administer medication?

- Can you bring your cat's bedding from home?

- What happens if you are late to pick up your cat?

- What vaccinations does the facility require?

- Will the facility provide you with references? (Always check references!)

Notes ·

· ·

· ·

· ·

· ·

· ·

· ·

BEHAVIOR

For the most part, cats do not act out so much as they just follow their natural drives. They usually have a very clear reason — hardwired into their brain — for everything they do. To this end, their behavior needs to be managed, or channeled, rather than broken. It's your job to find an appropriate outlet for your cat's behavior — and to protect certain items — so that the two of you can happily coexist in the same home. This seems very simple, but it's not always easy.

The following pages cover common behavioral issues in cats. However, if you and your cat cannot reach an accord, or if you encounter issues you do not think you can manage on your own, call in an expert to teach you how to redirect your cat's instincts in a less destructive manner. Don't put it off. Unlike dogs, which often require several lessons to correct problematic behavior, cat behavioral issues can frequently be resolved in one session.

CAT BEHAVIORISTS

The best way to find a cat behaviorist is to survey in-the-know cat-o-philes. Start with your vet, who will likely want to see your cat for a checkup to ensure that the behavior is not stemming from an underlying health issue before giving you a referral to a behaviorist. Cat rescuers, pet sitters, and groomers are also good resources for recommendations.

> **A GOOD CAT BEHAVIORIST**
> - *has been professionally trained or has apprenticed with an established cat behaviorist or trainer*
> - *regularly attends seminars and ongoing educational courses*
> - *treats both you and your cat with respect and is never physically or verbally abusive to your cat*
> - *is someone you feel comfortable working with*

aggression

PEOPLE-AGGRESIVE BEHAVIOR

Cats exhibit human-aggressive behavior for one of three reasons:

- They are afraid.
- They are playing and have not learned that biting and/or scratching is unacceptable.
- They are overstimulated, or whatever you are doing is causing them discomfort or pain.

PREVENTING PETTING-RELATED AGGRESSION

When a cat suddenly attacks while being petted, she is acting in self-defense. The petting, which may have started as a source of pleasure, is causing discomfort. If you watch closely, you will see that most cats give off several signs before "suddenly" attacking. To stop petting-related aggression, pay attention to how long your cat can be petted before showing signs of discomfort. Then make sure to stop petting your cat a few minutes before she reaches that limit.

Even cats with a very low tolerance for petting will usually let you scratch under their chin. Conversely, petting a cat on the stomach will almost always incite an attack from even the most docile cats. All of that said, everything in between falls under personal preference; pay attention so you can learn what your cat likes.

> **SIGNS THAT A CAT IS ABOUT TO ATTACK YOU**
> - *Twitching*
> - *Subtle movements*
> - *Flicking her tail*
> - *Watching you*

PREVENTING PLAYFUL AGGRESSION

- Play with your cat several times a day, using toys.

- Do not let your cat bite or scratch your fingers during play — ever!

A cat that attacks during play has gotten the message that you are fair game during play-time. Or she may simply be so bored that she will do anything, including stalking you as prey, to get your attention. In either case, your cat requires more play. It's up to you to teach your cat how to play appropriately.

If a cat has you in her jaws, do not pull away. Your cat will only bite down harder. Push your hand farther into her mouth, and she will release her grip on you.

DEALING WITH FEAR-RELATED AGGRESSION

A cat that exhibits aggression out of fear should be treated with great care. Provided your cat is neither injured nor in danger, simply leave her alone when she becomes frightened. If your cat is injured or is in danger, you will need to secure her, but do so with extreme caution, wrapping her up in a blanket to prevent bites and scratches. Even if you are not the cause of your cat's fear, she may still attack you. Causes of fear-related aggression include stressors, such as a trip to the vet, introducing a new animal to the house, a change in environment, or a trauma.

CAT-AGGRESSIVE BEHAVIOR

It is much easier to prevent a catfight than it is to break one up. If it looks as if two cats are about to go at it, distract them with tasty treats and favorite toys. If a catfight does break out, your options become much more limited. Jumping into the middle of a cat-fight or attempting to grab one of the cats will almost certainly guarantee that you will be bitten by one, if not both, of them. Your best bet is to startle them with a loud noise or squirt them with a water bottle or hose. Once the fight is broken up, separate the two cats as quickly as possible. If you have to pick them up, do so one at a time, using a blanket or towel to prevent them from biting or scratching you.

SIGNS THAT A CAT IS GETTING READY TO ATTACK ANOTHER CAT

- *Baring teeth; snarling*
- *Crouching down*
- *Flicking tail*
- *Hissing*
- *Pinning ears*
- *Raising the hair on her back and/or tail*

scratching

Cats are going to scratch. They do it both to sharpen their claws and to mark their territory. It is up to you to teach your cat what she is allowed to scratch and what is off limits. If you want your cat to stop scratching the furniture, carpet, or curtains, you must provide a more appealing alternative. While you are doing this, it helps to make the cat's preferred scratching spot as unappealing as possible.

If your cat has several scratching spots, you will need to get several scratching posts. Before you race out to buy them, however, figure out whether your cat prefers to scratch horizontally or vertically. If, like most people, you wait until she's damaged the furniture to address the issue, you should be able to figure this out pretty easily. Cats that scratch on the carpet will most likely be satisfied with a horizontal scratching post, whereas cats that scratch the sofa will most likely prefer a vertical post. And if your kitty likes to hang from the drapes like Tarzan, you might try a scratching object that hangs from the door.

TEACHING YOUR CAT TO STOP SCRATCHING IN A PARTICULAR SPOT

- Use an odor neutralizer to remove your cat's scent from her scratching spots. As long as she smells her scent, she'll return to the same spot to scratch.

- Make her spot as unappealing as possible.
  - Place clear two-sided tape on the scratching surface.
  - Lay a sheet over a sofa arm, and then place a can of pennies on top. If the sheet is not enough to deter your cat, the noise the pennies make when the can falls, should get her attention.
  - Block your cat's access to the scratching spot(s) by closing doors, putting obstacles in her path, etc.

- Teach your cat to use the scratching post. Place it as close as possible to her favorite scratching spot. If she's like most cats, she will not immediately take to it. Entice her by sprinkling catnip on it and by getting out toys and playing with your cat on and around the scratching post.

> When you were decorating your house, you probably didn't plan to have a scratching post as the focal point of your living room. The good news is that it doesn't need to remain there permanently. Once you have trained your cat to use the post, ever so gradually move it to a more desirable location.

DECLAWING

When all else fails, consider hiring a behaviorist to work with your cat to see if there is a way to solve your cat's scratching issues before even considering having her claws removed.

It's aggravating to have your cat shred your favorite furnishings or curtains in her efforts to maintain the perfect manicure. But be aware that declawing is not a minor procedure; don't consider it without exhausting all other alternatives.

Many veterinary facilities and humane societies are unconditionally opposed to declawing because of the pain that it causes cats. Nevertheless, while not condoning the procedure, some concede that declawing is unquestionably preferable to getting rid of your cat, or worse, having her euthanized.

For more information on the issues surrounding declawing, visit the San Francisco SPCA's Web site, www.sfspca.org, and enter declawing in the search box.

If you do decide that declawing is your only option, speak to your vet about the different choices. Your vet will most likely want to keep your cat a minimum of one night after the surgery. Once you take your cat home, be sure to follow your vet's instructions regarding follow-up care to prevent infection.

> *Do not declaw a cat that goes outdoors. Not only is a declawed cat severely hampered in self-defense, she also can no longer climb trees to escape predators. If you decide that your only option is to declaw your cat, then she absolutely must become an indoors-only cat.*

CLAW TRIMMING

Most cats are able to keep their claws sharp and short on their own. Unless you have convinced your cat to use a scratching post, she is most likely making use of your home décor to perform her self-manicure. If your cat isn't satisfied with a scratching post, keeping her claws trimmed will help minimize damage to your furnishings. Many vets will give you plastic tips that you can put on your cat's claws to help prevent punctures in your furniture. Depending on the strength and weave of the fabric, however, the tips only succeed in creating bigger, rounder holes.

If you want to be able to clip your cat's claws, start while your cat is still a kitten, when you have the best chance of desensitizing her to the process. Some cats will tolerate claw trimming better than others. If your cat has particularly sensitive claws, you will save yourself and your cat a lot of aggravation if you ask a groomer or vet tech to handle the job. A professional will be able to get the ordeal over with more quickly. And the truth is, if claw clipping is a truly negative experience for your cat, it's better that your cat not associate it with you.

HOW TO CLIP YOUR CAT'S CLAWS

- Make sure you have enough light to see clearly.
- Pick up your cat and hold her still — if necessary, have someone else hold and/or distract her. With one hand, hold a paw and gently press down on the top of each toe to extend the claw. The pink part of the claw is alive and you do not want to clip it. Anything beyond the pink part is considered dead. To be safe, aim to clip off no more than half of the dead part of the claw.
- Make each cut a smooth squeeze with the claw trimmers.
- When you are finished, always praise your cat and give her a healthy treat before you let her go.
- If your cat becomes agitated or restless, finish up that claw, give her a treat, and let her go. Forcing her to stay still will only make it that much harder to clip her claws the next time.

WHAT TO DO IF YOU CLIP TOO MUCH AND THE CLAW STARTS BLEEDING

- Press a tissue to the bottom of the claw.
- Apply a styptic powder (available at pet-supply stores) to the bottom of the claw.
- If bleeding doesn't stop after several minutes, contact your vet.

spraying

Unlike other forms of inappropriate elimination, cats spray to mark their territory. Cats remain standing while spraying; the target is a vertical surface, such as a wall or sofa arm. Although female cats do spray, it is more common for male cats, particularly unaltered males, to do so.

If your cat begins spraying, the sooner you address the problem, the better your chances of correcting it.

PREVENTING YOUR CAT FROM SPRAYING

- Use pheromone mist (available at most pet-supply stores).
- Play with your cat more often and/or for longer periods.
- Keep stress to a minimum.
- Block your cat's view of outdoor cats from the neighborhood.
- Prevent other cats from entering your property.
- Maintain a consistent routine.
- Clean all soiled areas as quickly as possible with an odor-neutralizing cleaner. Once you have thoroughly cleaned the area, use the spot for feeding and playing so your cat learns to associate it with something other than the desire to mark territory.
- If, and only if, you see the spraying happening, startle your cat with a squirt gun or by rattling a can of pennies. You have a very narrow window of opportunity here. If you squirt or startle after the fact, your cat will not associate this punishment with the spraying.

Yelling, striking or in any way terrorizing your cat will not break this (or any other) undesirable behavior. If anything, it will most likely cause your cat to spray more because of increased anxiety.

READ THIS BEFORE REDECORATING
Believe it or not, some cats are so upset by the smell of new furniture that they spray it to make it smell better. To prevent this from happening, wipe your cat down with a dry towel, and then wipe the towel over the new piece of furniture. If you have allergy sufferers in the house, instead of using the towel, substitute a sheet, towel, or piece of worn clothing from the cat's favorite person. You may want to keep the new furniture or carpet covered (or keep your cat out of the room for a couple of days) to allow time for the odor to dissipate, or at least blend in with the familiar scents that your cat is comfortable with.

separation anxiety

Believe it or not, independent as they appear, some cats do get separation anxiety when they are left alone or are separated from their owners and/or other pets in the house. If you find your cat exhibits anxiety when you leave or return, you can take steps to alleviate it.

ALLEVIATING SEPARATION ANXIETY

- Do not make a big deal about leaving. If possible, slip out while your cat is occupied. Making a big fuss over her just before you leave will only make her feel your absence more acutely.
- Keep your departure routine to a minimum. Your cat quickly learns to associate certain behaviors, such as rattling keys and moving at a quicker pace, with your departure.
- Hide kitty treats all over your cat's environment so she can go on a treasure hunt while you are gone. (When you get home, be sure to pick up any treats she didn't find.)
- Save favorite toys and put them out only right before you leave.
- Play with your cat and tire her out a half-hour or so before you leave so she will be ready for a nap.
- When you return, don't greet your cat for the first 10 minutes. Exuberant greetings or any type of punishment for misbehavior upon your return will only heighten your cat's anxiety about future homecomings.

SIGNS OF SEPARATION ANXIETY

- Vocalizing (whining)
- Soiling outside the litter box
- Soiling on your favorite items
- Remaining underfoot as you try to get out the door
- Refusing to eat while you are gone
- Vomiting
- Excessive self-grooming

Many of the signs of separation anxiety are also indicative of other illnesses. If your cat suddenly develops any of these symptoms, you should take her to your vet for an exam to rule out any underlying medical conditions that may be causing this behavior.

TREATING SEPARATION ANXIETY

- Talk to your vet about prescribing your cat a short course of anti-anxiety medication to help break the cycle.
- Consider hiring an animal behaviorist to help your cat work through the anxiety.

THROUGH THE YEARS/ADULT CATS
adult cat concerns & care

Although adult cats require little mainte-nance, taking the following measures will help your cat maintain optimum health.

- **ROUTINE CHECKUPS** By taking your cat in for annual exams, you have a better chance of catching disease and problems in the early stages.

- **DIET AND EXERCISE** By maintaining your cat's weight at a healthy level, you can prevent a whole host of problems later on. In addition to eating a healthy diet, your cat needs regular exercise. Set aside at least 15 minutes a day to play with her and get her moving.

- **DENTAL HYGIENE** Schedule regular teeth-cleaning appointments for your cat. Most vets will do teeth cleaning only under an-esthesia. Many pet-supply stores, however, now offer anesthesia-free teeth cleaning through outside providers.

> *To reduce the number of times your cat is anesthetized, consider getting her teeth cleaned any time she requires anesthesia for another procedure.*

- **FLEA AND TICK PREVENTION** If you have any pets in your household with access to the outdoors, administer a monthly flea preventative year-round in warmer cli-mates and from early spring through late fall in cooler climates. (For more on flea prevention, see page 59, in this section. For more information on ticks, see page 95 in **CAT HEALTH**.)

- **GROOMING** The amount of grooming your cat requires depends largely on the breed and fur length. Generally, cats with long hair need to be brushed daily, whereas cats with short hair can go a week before need-ing to be brushed.

- **NUTRITION** When it comes to cat food, you get what you pay for. The cheaper cat-food brands provide cats with about as much nutritional value as children receive from sugar-coated cereals.

- **PETTING** Each time you pet your cat, you should do a head-to-tail check, looking and feeling for anything unusual, including cuts, scars, lumps, swelling, odor, sores, tender areas, fleas, ticks, or anything else out of the ordinary.

- **VACCINATIONS** Get your cat vaccinated every one to three years, depending on what you and your vet agree upon.

- **VET CARE** If you notice anything unusual, check it out with your vet right away. Many vets will answer questions (or allow their vet techs to answer questions) over the phone if you're a regular client.

diet & exercise

HOW TO FIND A HEALTHY CAT FOOD FOR YOUR CAT

- Avoid cat foods that are available in supermarkets — look for a brand that is sold only in pet-supply stores and/or veterinary offices.
- Ask store owners or managers what their top picks are, as well as why they prefer one over another.
- Read the label:
  - Natural preservatives (Vitamin E) are better than chemical preservatives.
  - Avoid foods that list vegetables, especially corn, as the first ingredient. (Ingredients are listed in order, with primary ingredients listed first.) Choose a food that lists meat, poultry, or fish first, to ensure that your cat gets enough protein.
- **DO NOT** feed dog food to your cat. Cats have different dietary requirements from dogs, and dog food does not provide cats with adequate nutrition.

> *Do not supplement your cat's food with vitamins without consulting your vet first, as vitamins can be toxic. Many cat foods are already fortified with vitamins.*

> *When you change your cat's food, do so slowly, gradually mixing more and more of the new food in with the old food.*

OBESITY

There are several causes of obesity in cats, including:

- Too much food
- Not enough exercise
- Certain medications
- Dysfunction of the thyroid or pituitary gland

Obesity causes numerous diseases, including:

- Diabetes
- Arthritis
- Liver and heart disease

TIPS FOR HELPING YOUR CAT LOSE WEIGHT

- Take your cat in for a checkup so your vet can rule out any underlying medical conditions that might be causing or contributing to the obesity. While you're there, consult your vet about the best way to help your cat lose weight.
- Monitor your cat's portions and/or consider changing to a lower-calorie cat food.
- Do not drastically reduce the amount of food you feed your cat—it's best for your cat to lose excess weight in a slow, healthy manner.
- Cut out all table scraps and treats.
- Increase your cat's playtime and play games with that require your cat to exert energy.

Free-choice feeding means leaving cat food out at all times for your cat to graze on, so she can eat whenever she feels like it. If this is the way you feed your cat and your cat is overweight, consider changing to a lower-calorie cat food and/or increasing your cat's daily exercise regimen. If your cat is still not losing weight, you should consider gradually switching your cat to an established feeding schedule.

 Pay attention to your cat's weight as well as to food and water intake. Sudden changes in your cat's appetite and thirst level are often one of the first signs of a health issue. Consult your vet as soon as possible to rule out any acute, life-threatening conditions. A sudden or extreme gain or loss in weight is also grounds for speaking to your vet as soon as possible.

dental hygiene

Cats are just as susceptible as people are to gingivitis and periodontal disease. And just as in people, periodontal disease in cats can lead to serious health conditions, including heart disease, kidney and liver dysfunction, and tooth loss and abscesses.

SIGNS OF PERIDONTAL DISEASE

- Bad breath
- Tartar buildup, especially around the gum line
- Gums that bleed and/or are sensitive to touch
- Puffy gums
- Red gums

In many cases, before you can start an effective dental hygiene program at home, your cat will require a professional dental cleaning, performed by a veterinarian under anesthesia.

PREVENTING PERIODONTAL DISEASE

- Feed your cat dry — as opposed to wet — food.
- Brush your cat's teeth on a regular basis — at least every other day.
- Give your cat treats specifically designed to help protect your cat against periodontal disease.
- Have your vet do an annual dental exam on your cat.
- When indicated, have your vet give your cat a thorough dental cleaning under anesthesia.
- Have your vet remove decaying teeth.

> If your cat has to go under anesthesia for another procedure, consider scheduling ultrasonic teeth cleaning at the same time.

HOW TO BRUSH YOUR CAT'S TEETH AND KEEP YOUR FINGERS

Depending on how acquiescent your cat is (and let's face it — most cats aren't at all), you will need to get your cat used to you sticking something in her mouth. The best way to do this is, of course, with bribery.

- Douse your finger with something savory (chicken broth, tuna water) and let your cat lick it off your fingers, gently rubbing your fingers on her front teeth/gums. (It may take several attempts before your cat is comfortable with this.)
- Using a toothbrush/sponge and toothpaste made specifically for cats, begin brushing your cat's teeth. (You may not get very far the first few times, but just keep at it.) If she doesn't come around after several attempts, try a different-flavored toothpaste.
- Keep your tooth-brushing sessions short and sweet.
- Always praise your cat while you're brushing her teeth and give her a healthy treat when you're done.
- Do not use human toothpaste! It's not meant to be swallowed and will make your cat sick.

WHEN TO PUT AWAY THE BREATH MINTS AND SEE THE VET

- When your cat's breath smells fruity or sweet. This odor is an indicator of diabetes.
- When your cat's breath is unusually foul. This odor is an indicator of infection, advanced tooth decay, advanced gum disease, or serious internal health problems.

fleas & mites

Fleas are the number-one cause of allergies in cats. It goes without saying that any cat with access to the outdoors should be regularly treated for fleas. Even indoor cats, however, should be on a flea-prevention program if you have other animals that go outdoors. Frontline, Advantage, and Revolution are the three top brands; each offers user-friendly topical treatments.

> *Do not use canine flea-control products on your cat! They are incredibly toxic for cats, and can cause everything from neurological problems to death. Use only products specifically made for cats.*

The best way to prevent a flea infestation is to consistently administer flea-prevention medication to all your pets, as directed by the manufacturer. If an animal brings fleas into the house, you can pretty much figure that all your other pets, as well as the house itself, will become infested.

If, despite your best efforts, your home becomes infested with fleas, you have several options. The most important thing you need to do is to act fast.

RIDDING YOUR PETS AND HOUSE OF FLEAS

Depending on the severity of the situation, consider doing any or all of the following:

- Treat all your pets with a flea-prevention medication. Treatment options include topical ointments, dips, and shampoos.
- Vacuum all rugs, carpets, and upholstery.
- Wash all flea-exposed bedding, clothing, and linens in soapy hot water.

- Set off a flea bomb or fogger. (Be sure to keep people and animals out of the treated area for the designated time period!)
- Use a flea powder.
- Bring in a professional to de-flea your house.
- Mow your grass as short as possible and treat your lawn with an insecticide.

FLEA BOMBING

When flea bombing your home, close off any rooms that have not been infested and remove all people and animals from the house for the designated time period.

Flea foggers/bombs are incredibly toxic, which is why they are so effective in killing fleas. Before you fog your house, take the following precautions:

- *In the kitchen, completely cover or remove all food, utensils, dishware, glasses, etc.*
- *In the bathroom, completely cover or remove all tissue, toilet paper, towels, washcloths, toiletries, toothbrushes, hairbrushes, makeup, etc.*
- *In the bedroom, remove all bedding and pillows, and completely cover or remove all clothes.*

> *Remember to get a medication that's made for the animal. If you have several kinds of animals, you'll need several different medications.*

MITES

If you can see coffee grounds–type particles in your cat's ear, you're most likely seeing ear mites. Once you've spotted the telltale coffee grounds, do not be surprised if you find that your cat also has a skin rash.

TREATING MITES

Because of their microscopic size, the actual mites are hard to see, and therefore tough to treat at home.

TREATMENT REQUIRES

- A trip to the vet for an ear cleaning. (If your vet has okayed it and given you instructions on how to clean the ears, you can sometimes do this at home.)
- Administering a topical ointment to kill the mites.
- Administering a flea preventative to kill any mites that may be lurking in your cat's hair outside of the ear.

AVOIDING AN IN-HOME EAR MITE EPIDEMIC

If any of your pets get ear mites, treat all your animals. Ask your vet whether to bring in all of your animals or whether he or she, or a vet tech, can show you how to clean the ears and administer the ointment at home. You definitely want to get rid of the mites as quickly as possible, so when in doubt, take all your animals to the vet.

more on grooming

Provided you have the time and energy, as well as your cat's cooperation, there is no reason you can't perform many grooming duties yourself. You'll have a much easier time grooming your cat if you were able to get your cat used to these procedures while she was still a kitten. (Treats also help.) If grooming is particularly stressful for your cat, you may want to enlist a professional groomer. The last thing you want is for your cat to as-

sociate you negatively with grooming. (For more information on **FULL-SERVICE GROOMING**, see page 45 in this section.)

ANAL GLAND EXPRESSION

Young, healthy cats should not need to have their anal glands expressed, but many older cats need to have the procedure done. Unless your vet has shown you how to express your cat's anal glands and has said it is all right for you to do so on your own, do not do it at home.

AROMATHERAPY

Unless an aromatherapy product (shampoo, oil, or the like) is specifically approved for use on a cat, do not use it. Many oils and shampoos (all-natural and otherwise) are toxic to cats.

BATHING

This is where groomers really earn their money. While some cats (a very select few) do not mind this process, other cats will scratch and bite you every step of the way. Fortunately, unless they have gotten into something, cats rarely need a full bath. If you do decide to bathe your cat at home, wear a long-sleeved thick shirt and gloves to help prevent getting scratched and/or bitten.

CLAW TRIMMING

For instructions on how to trim your cat's claws, see **CLAW TRIMMING** on page 53.

EAR CLEANING

Cats do not need to have their ears routinely cleaned. Unless your vet has shown you how to clean your cat's ears and has said it's all right for you to clean them, do not attempt to do so on your own, as they can be easily damaged. Also, if your cat needs her ears cleaned, she most likely has an ear infection that your vet needs to diagnose and treat.

TREATING MATTED FUR

If your cat has short hair, matted fur is not an issue. If you have a long-haired cat, though, be sure to brush her frequently so that mats don't form. If they do form, you may be able to cut smaller ones out on your own. However, you need to be absolutely certain that you are cutting hair and not skin. If your cat's hair becomes heavily matted, you will need to get a groomer or vet to do the job.

older cat concerns

Acknowledging the signs that your cat is growing old is about as much fun as finding your first gray hair. The earlier you address the issue, the more you can do to sustain her quality of life and prevent, or at least delay, disease.

Generally speaking, a cat is considered to be "senior" when she is 12 years old. By 15 years, your cat is considered aged. Ask your vet when it would be a good idea to start screening your cat for geriatric health issues.

TIPS FOR MAINTAINING YOUR OLDER CAT'S QUALITY OF LIFE

- **ACUPUNCTURE AND CHIROPRACTIC** Consider scheduling treatments for your cat to help alleviate arthritis and chronic pain. (For more information on acupuncture or chiropractic, see specific topics in **CAT HEALTH**.)
- **DENTAL HYGIENE** Brush your cat's teeth and schedule regular teeth-cleaning appointments. Tooth decay and gum disease can lead to a slew of other health problems. (For more information, see 58 in this section.)
- **DIET** Watch your cat's weight! As cats age, their metabolism slows, which means they burn fewer calories and require less food.
- **EXERCISE** Modify — but don't cut out — your cat's exercise regimen. Playing with her daily will do much to keep her young.

- **GROOMING** Brush and groom your cat regularly to help her maintain a healthy coat and prevent hairballs. Regularly check to see if she needs her claws trimmed. As they age, many cats lose the ability to effectively groom their coats and/or maintain their claws.
- **KNOWING YOUR CAT** Be aware of, and be on the lookout for, illnesses and issues that are typical of your cat's breed.
- **IMPROVING ACCESSIBILITY**
  - Consider relocating your cat's litter box and food/water dishes if your cat begins to have trouble reaching them.
  - Consider purchasing the following:
  - A litter box with shorter sides
  - A ramp or pet stairs to help your cat get on and off furniture
  - Skidproof carpeting to prevent your cat from injuring herself on slippery surfaces and stairs
- **MASSAGE** Give your cat regular massage treatments to improve circulation and ease tension, aches, and pains. If you do not want to pay for regular massage treatments, take a class or schedule an animal massage therapist for a one-time visit to teach you how to work on your cat yourself.
- **NUTRITION** Feed your cat high-quality food to help maintain optimal health.
- **ROUTINE CHECKUPS** Increase the frequency of your cat's routine exam to every six to eight months.
- **SUPPLEMENTS** Consider giving your cat certain supplements, and check with your vet for proper dosage information:
  - Glucosamine sulfate and chondroitin (for arthritis)
  - Vitamin and mineral supplements (for overall health)
  - Omega-3 fatty acids (for coat)
  - Glycerin (for eyes)
- **VACCINATIONS** Ask your vet about the risks and benefits of stopping vaccinations altogether (if your cat is over 10 years old).

Cat Concerns & Care | OLDER CAT CONCERNS

WHEN TO SEE YOUR VET

Unfortunately, despite preventive measures, older cats are more prone to illness and disease. If your cat has any of the following symptoms, schedule an appointment with your vet as soon as possible. These symptoms are not a normal result of the aging process.

- Abnormal swelling or lumps
- Sores that don't heal
- Eye discharge
- Nasal discharge
- Bleeding or discharge from any body opening
- Stiffness or lameness
- Diarrhea or vomiting that lasts longer than a day
- Difficulty defecating
- Difficulty urinating
- Increased urination and/or change in urine color
- Inappropriate elimination and/or spraying
- Refusal to use a clean litter box
- Difficulty breathing
- Excessive panting

- Difficulty eating or swallowing
- Loss of appetite
- Weight loss
- Increased thirst/water intake
- Difficulty or reluctance to do routine activities
- Exhaustion and/or apathy
- Sudden change in activity level
- Unusual aggression
- Change in sleep patterns
- Confusion
- Excessive grooming
- Offensive body odor
- Offensive breath
- Offensive ear odor or dirty ears
- Overgrown and/or brittle claws
- Poor coat condition
  - Bald spots
  - Dull in appearance
  - Mats
  - Excessive shedding

> *For information on specific conditions, diseases, and illnesses, see* **CAT HEALTH** **(CHAPTER 3)**.

Notes . . . .

. . . .

. . . .

. . . .

. . . .

. . . .

. . . .

when cats go to heaven/pet loss support

The disparity between our pets' lifespan and our own is one of the great injustices in this world. Losing a pet is a very sad, sometimes devastating, experience. Many people do not realize how much they will be affected until it happens. If you are too overcome with grief to deal with the logistics, ask your vet's office if they can help or if they can recommend someone who can. Many veterinarians' offices will handle all the arrangements for you, including picking up your pet and having her cremated or buried. It may seem like a morbid thing to do, but it might be a good idea to ask in advance if your vet's office will perform any of these tasks for you. Then, when the need arises, you will know to what degree you can count on your vet to help.

EUTHANASIA

The decision to put an animal to sleep is one of the most difficult decisions a pet owner must make. The fact that it may be the most humane thing to do does not make it any easier. You may want to consult with your vet, and perhaps someone else you trust, and ask for help determining if it is the right time and the right thing to do for your cat.

If you decide euthanasia is the best thing to do, consider arranging for a vet to come to your house. This way, your cat can spend her final moments in the comfort of her home. Ask your vet to prescribe a sedative for your cat that you can give her prior to your vet's arrival. If your vet will not perform in-home euthanasia, he or she should be able to supply you with the name of a vet who does provide this service.

FINAL ARRANGEMENTS

A reputable pet funeral home or crematorium should treat you and your cat with compas-

sion and respect as well as provide you with options that fit your financial situation. You may want to make arrangements in advance so that when the time comes, you will not have to worry about deciding what to do. Again, your vet is likely the best resource for information on reputable funeral homes and crematoriums. Following is a list of resources that can help you with your plans.

PET LOSS BOOKS

Many pet lovers have found the following books useful in helping them come to terms with losing their cat:

Coping with the Loss of a Pet: A Gentle Guide for All Who Love a Pet by Christina M. Lemieux (Reading, Pa.: W. R. Clark, 1991).

Coping with Sorrow on the Loss of Your Pet, 2nd edition, by Moira K. Anderson (Loveland, Colo.: Alpine Publications, 1996).

The Loss of a Pet by Wallace Sife, rev. ed. (New York: Howell Book House, 1998).

Pet Loss: A Thoughtful Guide for Adults and Children by Herbert Nieberg (New York: Harper & Row, 1996).

PET LOSS HOTLINES

Sometimes even the most caring and well-intentioned friends and family members cannot grasp the degree of sorrow you feel from losing your cat. Following are a list of pet loss hotlines with volunteers trained specifically to help people work through their feelings surrounding the loss of their companion.

ASPCA NATIONAL PET LOSS HOTLINE
- Hours: 24/7
- Counselors: Volunteers
- Phone: (800) 946-4646
  - Press 140 7211, then your own phone number.
- E-mail: stephaniel@aspca.org
- Web site: www.aspca.org

UNIVERSITY OF ILLINOIS,
COLLEGE OF VETERINARY MEDICINE

C.A.R.E. Helpline for Companion Animal
  Related Emotions

- Hours: Sun., Tues. & Thurs.: 7 p.m.–9 p.m. CST
- Counselors: Volunteer veterinary students
- Phone: (217) 244-2273
- E-mail: griefhelp@cvm.uiuc.edu
- Web Site: www.cvm.uiuc.edu/care

UNIVERSITY OF CALIFORNIA,
DAVIS SCHOOL OF VETERINARY MEDICINE

Pet Loss Support Hotline

- Hours: Mon.–Fri: 6:30 p.m.–9:30 p.m. PST
- Counselors: Volunteer veterinary students
- Toll-Free Hotline: (800) 565-1526
- Business Office Hotline: (530) 752-3602
- Web Site: www.vetmed.ucdavis.edu/petloss

COMPANION ANIMAL ASSOCIATION OF
ARIZONA INC. PET GRIEF SUPPORT SERVICE

- Hours: 24/7
- Counselors: Trained volunteers
- Hotline: (602) 995-5885
- Office: (602) 258-3306
- Other services: Support groups, literature
- Notes: Long-distance calls returned collect
- Web Site: www.caaainc.org/petgriefsupport.htm

CORNELL UNIVERSITY,
COLLEGE OF VETERINARY MEDICINE

Pet Loss Support Hotline

- Hours: Tues.–Thurs: 6 p.m.–9 p.m. EST
- Counselors: Volunteer veterinary students
- Hotline: (607) 253-3932
- Web site: www.vet.cornell.edu/public/
  petloss/

MICHIGAN STATE UNIVERSITY,
COLLEGE OF VETERINARY MEDICINE

Pet Loss Support Program

- Hours: Tues.–Thurs: 6:30 p.m.–9:30 p.m. EST
- Counselors: Volunteer veterinary students
- Hotline: (517) 432-2696

- E-mail: EWalshaw@pilot.msu.edu
- Other services: Monthly support group run by
  psychologist or social worker
- Web Site: http://cvm.msu.edu/petloss/petloss.htm

TUFTS UNIVERSITY,
CUMMINGS SCHOOL OF VETERINARY
MEDICINE

Pet Loss Support Hotline

- Hours: Mon.–Fri: 6 p.m.–9 p.m. EST
- Hotline: (508) 839-7966
- Web site: www.tufts.edu/vet/petloss/

PET LOSS RESOURCES ON THE WEB

THE ASSOCIATION FOR PET LOSS AND
BEREAVEMENT (APLB)

- Web site: www.aplb.org
- Phone: (718) 382-0960
- Services: Chat rooms, nationwide database
  that includes pet cemeteries and lawyers spe-
  cializing in pet-related wrongful-action cases,
  as well as hotline, counselor, and support-
  group information

GRIEF HEALING

- Web site: www.griefhealing.com
- Services: General loss as well as pet loss re-
  source, tips for helping children cope, links
- E-mail: tousleym@aol.com

RAINBOW BRIDGE

- Web site: www.rainbowbridge.com
- E-mail: friends@rainbowsbridge.com
- Services: Pet loss forums, questions to help
  'your work through your grief, chat rooms,
  one-on-one counseling, tributes, euthanasia
  advice, virtual memorial ($25), tips for helping
  children cope, links

DELTA SOCIETY

- Hours: Mon. - Fri.: 8:30 a.m. - 4:30 p.m. (PST)
- Web site: www.deltasociety.org
- Services: List of Web sites, hotlines, counsel-
  ors, and support groups

Chapter 3

 CAT HEALTH

Though cats come with nine lives, hazards to their well-being lurk everywhere, and it's important that an owner be aware of common conditions and emergencies. This section offers advice on many health issues, from allergies and feline viruses to choking, falls, and snakebites.

in this chapter

- Abscesses
- Acupuncture
- Allergies
- Appetite Change
- Arthritis
- Bee Stings
- Cancer
- Car Sickness
- Cataracts
- Chiropractic
- Choking
- Diabetes
- Ear Infections
- Falls
- Feline Cognitive Dysfunction (FCD)
- Feline Immunodeficiency Virus (FIV)
- Feline Infectious Peritonitis (FIP)
- Feline Leukemia Virus (FeLV)
- Feline Lower Urinary Tract Disease (FLUTD)
- Fleabites
- Frostbite
- Heartworm Disease
- Heatstroke
- Homeopathy
- Hookworms
- Hypothermia
- Incontinence
- Lyme Disease
- Panting
- Poisons
- Puncture Wounds
- Ringworms
- Roundworms
- Shock
- Skunks
- Snakebites
- Tick Bites
- West Nile Virus

> **WARNING!**
>
> In no way is the information in this book, and particularly this section, meant to replace emergency and/or routine veterinary care. The content of this book is designed for informational purposes only.
>
> If your cat requries medical attention, contact your vet or animal emergency facility immediately!

abscesses

> See **PUNCTURE WOUNDS** on page 89 in this chapter.

acupuncture

The ancient healing art of acupuncture dates back over 3,000 years. Though considered alternative therapy, acupuncture is becoming increasingly popular among vets, many of whom claim to observe increased alertness, playfulness, and better overall health in treated patients. Predominantly used to treat horses and dogs, acupuncture is slowly becoming more commonly used on cats.

Based on the idea that infirmity blocks the "chi," or life force, acupuncture involves the placement of fine needles in specific points along the body. The goal is to balance your cat's energy system by dispersing blockages, which decreases inflammation and alleviates pain, helping restore optimum health. Even if your cat is not exhibiting overt signs of illness, the acupuncturist can examine her energy points and check them for blockages or misalignment. Areas that may become problematic in the future can be targeted and treated, minimizing or possibly even preventing future pain or infirmity.

Animals undergoing acupuncture often sink into a restful, sleepy state, most likely because of the increased endorphin levels the treatment is said to produce. Acupuncture does not always provide immediate relief, however. Your cat may require several treatments before showing signs of improvement.

HEALTH ISSUES THAT MAY BE TREATED WITH ACUPUNCTURE

- Allergies
- Anxiety
- Arthritis
- Gastrointestinal problems
- Kidney problems
- Seizures
- Spinal disorders

To find a licensed veterinary acupuncturist in your area, visit the Web site of the American Academy of Veterinary Acupuncture, www.aava.org.

allergies

ALLERGIES			
	AIRBORNE	**CONTACT**	**FOOD**
COMMON ALLERGENS	• air freshener • cat litter • dust • household cleaning sprays • perfume • pollen	• carpet • fleas* • household cleaning products • newspaper ink • plants	• dairy • meat • grains
SIGNS	• labored breathing • coughing • skin lesions/scabs	• skin inflammation (under armpits, inside back legs, ears, chin) • rash, bumps, or blemishes • skin lesions/scabs	• skin inflammation/lesions (face, ears, chin)
TREATMENT	• antihistamines or steroids	• antihistamines or steroids • skin patch testing	• food-elimination diet
PREVENTION	• minimize your cat's exposure to allergens by keeping her out of rooms where allergens exist • eliminate allergens from her environment • purchase an air filter/purifier	• minimize your cat's exposure to allergens by keeping her out of rooms where allergens exist • eliminate allergens from her environment	• always feed your cat in a clean stainless steel bowl • feed your cat a diet free of artificial flavors, dyes, and preservatives • change your cat's diet frequently but gradually by mixing old food with new food to challenge her immune system

* For more information on fleas, see **FLEAS**, on page 59 in **CAT CONCERNS & CARE**.

**FOOD ALLERGIES —
FOOD ELIMINATION DIET**

If your cat is showing symptoms of food allergies, you may need to put your cat on a food-elimination diet to determine the allergen. (You should implement this diet only under the supervision of a veterinarian.) For this diet to be successful, you need to be hypervigilant about preventing your cat from eating any food that is not on the diet. And during this diet, make sure your cat drinks only filtered water — block your cat's access to leaky faucets and toilet bowls. Also, use only a clean stainless steel or porcelain bowl to feed your cat. Do not use plastic bowls, which tend to harbor bacteria.

The first thing you need to do is eliminate the allergen. You can do this by putting your cat on a protein/carbohydrate diet. A few cat-food manufacturers now offer hypoallergenic foods, which you can purchase at most quality pet-food stores. If you want to make the food yourself, combine boiled chicken and lamb with rice.

If your cat's food was causing the allergy, all symptoms should disappear within two weeks. At this point you have two choices: You can avoid all the ingredients in your cat's original food indefinitely. Or you can do an eight-week test on each ingredient, introducing only one new ingredient at a time, until you find the allergen.

appetite change

A dramatic change in appetite, thirst, or weight is symptomatic of many diseases. If you notice such a change, take your cat to the vet for a proper diagnosis.

arthritis

Arthritis is the term used to describe any number of degenerative joint diseases; symptoms include pain, swelling, and stiffness.

PREVENTABLE? TO SOME EXTENT
See Older Cat Concerns & Care, page 59, for more information on measures you can take that will help alleviate your cat's arthritis.

SIGNS OF ARTHRITIS
- Apathy
- Irritability
- Decreased energy
- Difficulty or hesitation getting into or out of the litter box
- Difficulty or hesitation jumping onto a bed or high perches
- Difficulty or hesitation leaning down to eat or drink
- Limping
- Stiffness
- Slowed movement
- Weight gain

TREATABLE? YES
- Prescription anti-inflammatory medications. You can use anti-inflammatories in the short term for severe flare-ups. Talk to your vet about potential side effects before starting this or any medications.
- Acupuncture
- Glucosamine-chondroitin supplements. You can give your pet these supplements over the long term to help promote healing and reduce degeneration. They are not effective for severe flare-ups.

> *Under no circumstances should you give your cat aspirin, ibuprofen (Advil®, Motrin®), naproxen (Aleve®), or acetaminophen (Tylenol®). These medications are very toxic to your cat.*

bee stings

Cats are usually protected from bees and wasps by their coat. However, the nose, mouth, and paws are vulnerable.

SIGNS YOUR CAT HAS BEEN STUNG

- Biting at paws
- Extreme agitation
- Scratching at mouth, nose, or face
- Shaking head
- Swelling
- Shock (For more information, see **SHOCK** on page 91 in this section.)

WHAT TO DO IF YOUR CAT GETS STUNG

- Wrap your cat in a large towel or blanket so she doesn't scratch or bite you when you examine her.
- If you find the stinger, remove it ASAP with a pair of tweezers.
- Gently pat down the affected area with a liquid paste made from baking soda and water.
- Put an ice pack on the area.
- Contact your vet.
- Do not panic if you can't find the stinger. Cats are often able to dislodge it on their own.

CONVENTIONAL TREATMENT

 Consult your vet for dosage information.

- Children's Benadryl® (antihistamine)
- Topical cortisone cream to reduce itching

ALTERNATIVE TREATMENT

 Consult your alternative vet for dosage information.

- Topical calendula cream to reduce itching
- Homeopathic apis to reduce the swelling
- Rescue Remedy® to treat shock

> *If your cat appears to have been stung in the mouth, call your vet or animal emergency facility ASAP. A sting in the mouth can cause an obstruction of the airway, and your cat may require an antihistamine or steroid shot.*

cancer

Unfortunately, cats can get cancer just as humans can.

COMMON TYPES OF CANCER IN CATS

- **Lymphoma.** Caused by infection with the feline leukemia virus, lymphoma is diagnosed in cats more frequently than any other type of cancer, and more often in cats than dogs or people.
- **Skin cancer.** Caused by exposure to direct sunlight, this type of cancer is most common in cats with white fur (especially on their ears) who are exposed to direct sunlight.

SIGNS YOUR CAT MAY HAVE CANCER

- Abnormal swelling
- Bleeding or discharge from any body opening
- Sores that won't heal
- Chronic lameness and/or stiffness
- Difficulty breathing
- Loss of appetite
- Difficulty eating and/or swallowing
- Unexplained weight loss
- Difficulty urinating and/or defecating
- Offensive breath or body odor
- Unexplained exhaustion

PREVENTABLE? **TO SOME EXTENT**

- Do not overvaccinate your cat. Always ask your vet where your cat received the vaccine. Watch the spot for any lumps or swelling.
- Protect your cat from infectious diseases, such as FeLV.
- Watch and/or feel for abnormal lumps when petting and grooming your cat.
- Spay your female cat before she goes through her first heat.
- Neuter your male cat before he reaches nine months.
- Make sure your cat receives a healthy, well-balanced diet, gets plenty of exercise, and maintains a healthy weight.
- Keep cats with white fur (especially on their ears) indoors and out of direct sunlight.

CAUSES

- Environmental toxins
- Genetics
- Infectious diseases
- Prolonged sun exposure

TREATABLE? **TO SOME EXTENT**

Depending on the type and progress of the cancer, your vet may call for any of the following treatments to be used in any combination:

- Surgery (to remove a tumor)
- Biopsy
- Radiation therapy
- Chemotherapy
- Pain management

When deciding which treatment course to take, it is important to consider the quality of your cat's life, rather than simply using all means at your disposal to prolong your cat's life as long as possible.

> *Alternative therapies, such as acupuncture, are much more effective in preventing than treating cancer.*

car sickness

SIGNS THAT YOUR CAT MAY VOMIT

- Excessive drooling
- Apathy

WHAT TO DO IF YOUR CAT GETS CARSICK

- Crack a window or turn the air conditioning up. Make sure there is plenty of air blowing into your cat's crate or carrier.
- If you can do so safely, stop the car and turn the engine off for a few minutes.

HOW TO HELP PREVENT CAR SICKNESS

- Feed your cat three hours before your trip — then remove all food.
- Help your cat adjust to the car by taking her on frequent short trips.
- Ask your vet to prescribe a medication for motion sickness. Be sure to give it to your cat early enough for it to have time to take effect.

cataracts

Cataracts, defined as cloudiness of the eye lens, appear as a white coating or yellowish film covering the pupil. The most common form of cataracts are senile cataracts, which usually affect both eyes at once. When younger cats develop a cataract, it is usually the result of a trauma to the eye.

PREVENTABLE? **TO SOME EXTENT**

- Senile cataracts or cataracts brought on by diabetes are not preventable. However, supplementing your pet's diet with vitamins E and C will help slow the development and progression of cataracts.

- Keeping your cat indoors will greatly decrease her chances of getting a single cataract through trauma to the eye.

TREATABLE? YES

Cataracts can be removed surgically by a veterinarian. This treatment, however, is a recourse only when a cat has gone completely blind.

> *If your cat has cataracts, be sure to keep her litter box and food dishes in their usual places. If you must move them around, be sure to show your cat where you've moved them.*

chiropractic

Chiropractic treatment is the physical manipulation of the spinal column and musculoskeletal system, with the goal of producing optimal balance in the body. While a series of chiropractic treatments is frequently recommended, a chiropractic adjustment often provides a cat with instant pain relief and increased mobility.

SKELETAL SYSTEM AND JOINTS

When all the vertebrae are in alignment, the cat is capable of pain-free movement and flexibility. When one or more of the joints fall out of alignment, the joints can become stiff or sore, decreasing the cat's mobility.

MUSCULAR SYSTEM

When joints are out of alignment, they put undue pressure on the muscles, causing spasms, knots, and — over time — degeneration. Conversely, weak muscles that do not properly support the skeletal system can cause joints to fall out of alignment.

NERVOUS SYSTEM

Nerves direct communication between the brain and all other areas of the body. When one or more joints fall out of alignment, the nerves can become blocked and/or pinched.

CHIROPRACTIC TREATMENT

Chiropractic treatment can be extremely beneficial for cats suffering from discomfort in the skeletal, muscular, or nervous system. All three systems are so interconnected that adjusting one (the skeletal system) almost always positively affects the other two (the muscular and nervous systems).

Chiropractic treatment is often helpful in treating animals with the following conditions or symptoms:

- Arthritis
- Joint pain
- Injury or trauma to the tail, back, or legs
- Misalignment of the tail, back, legs, neck, hips, and/or head
- Hesitation or difficulty going up or down stairs
- Hesitation or difficulty jumping, or difficulty landing from a jump
- Unexplained irritability, usually a sign of pain

choking

SIGNS OF CHOKING

A choking cat may exhibit any of the following signs:

- Distress
- Pawing at face
- Blue tongue
- Difficulty breathing
- Drooling
- Glazed eyes
- Gagging
- Loss of consciousness

POTENTIALLY FATAL? YES

PREVENTABLE? TO AN EXTENT

- Securely lock your garbage cans so your cat cannot forage through your trash for tasty treats.
- Consult your vet immediately if your cat gets stung in the mouth by a spider, bee, or insect.
- Do not leave any type of thread, string, or yarn lying about for your cat to discover (Be especially vigilant about putting away sewing, knitting, gift-wrapping supplies, etc.).
- Do not give your cat chicken bones (especially uncooked).

TREATABLE? YES

- Wrap your cat in a large towel or blanket so she doesn't scratch or bite you as you examine her and attempt to remove the object.
- If you can see the object that is causing your cat to choke, pull the cat's tongue forward and then attempt to remove it with either your fingers or a pair of blunt-tipped tweezers. Do not attempt to remove an object you cannot see!

> **WARNING!**
>
> If your cat has swallowed any type of thread, string, or yarn, do not pull on it! Take your cat to your vet or animal emergency facility ASAP!

- You should take your cat to see the vet even if you are able to dislodge the object on your own, as your cat may have sustained internal injuries either from her attempts to swallow the object or in your efforts to remove it.
- Call your vet or animal emergency facility immediately if you cannot remove the object. They can advise you whether you should rush your cat in for treatment or attempt to dislodge the object yourself. If they recommend that you attempt to dislodge the item yourself, you have two choices:
  - Using the heel of your hand, hit your cat between her shoulder blades.
  - Perform the Heimlich maneuver on your cat:
- With one hand, hold your cat under her arms to keep her still.
- Using either your fist or the heel of your other hand, press in and up on your cat's abdomen, several times in quick succession.
- Check your cat's mouth to see if the object has been dislodged.
- Clear any debris from her mouth.
- If you fail to dislodge the object, rush your cat to the nearest animal emergency facility immediately.

diabetes

Most common in older and/or overweight cats, diabetes can be life-threatening if not properly treated.

POTENTIALLY FATAL? **YES**

PREVENTABLE? **TO AN EXTENT**
Make sure your cat maintains a healthy weight through diet and exercise.

SIGNS OF DIABETES
- Excessive hunger and thirst
- Frequent and/or inappropriate urination
- Weight loss

TREATABLE? **YES**
- Administer insulin injections or oral medication twice a day.
- Monitor your cat to make sure she is getting enough insulin. There are several ways to do this (see below), which vary in complexity and cost. Talk to your vet about your options before you decide how to proceed.
  - Monitor your cat's water intake and urination.
  - Use a dipstick.
  - Test your cat's blood (at home or at the vet).
- Feed your cat a healthy diet that is high in fiber. (Ask your vet for a recommendation.)

 The amount of insulin your cat needs is based on the amount of food consumed. You should not adjust one without adjusting the other one.

For more information on diabetes in your cat, check out the Feline Diabetes Web site at www.felinediabetes.com.

**HYPOGLYCEMIA:
TOO MUCH OF A GOOD THING
CAN BE DEADLY**
One of the biggest concerns for diabetic cats is hypoglycemia (low blood sugar), which is brought on by giving a cat too much insulin.

SIGNS OF HYPOGLYCEMIA
- Chills/fever
- Excessive hunger/indifference to food
- Apathy
- Exhaustion
- Inability to focus
- Unsteadiness
- Twitching
- Seizures
- Confusion
- Coma

TREATMENT
- If your cat is unconscious, rub small amounts of corn syrup on her gums, along the side of the mouth. Do not put corn syrup inside her mouth, as it could pose a choking hazard.
- If your cat is conscious, apply the corn syrup inside her mouth, along the side, using your finger.
- As soon as your cat is alert, feed her normal food or treats. If necessary, mix the corn syrup in with the food or treats.
- Monitor your cat for the rest of the day/evening.

Contact your vet as soon as possible to discuss follow-up care, including whether you should bring your cat in to be examined and/or adjust your cat's next insulin dose.

ear infections

SIGNS YOUR CAT HAS AN EAR INFECTION
- Bacteria or yeast in ear(s)
- Coffee ground–type particles in ear(s)
- Discharge (wet or dry) in ear(s)
- Foreign objects (debris, dirt, mites, ticks) in ear(s)
- Offensive odor emanating from ear(s)
- Loss of hearing and/or balance
- Refusal to let you touch her ears
- Ear scratching
- Shaking and/or tilting her head

TREATABLE? YES

If your cat has an ear infection, your vet will need to examine your cat in order to prescribe the appropriate medicine. Treatment usually involves administering a topical ointment to the infected ear. In severe cases, your cat may require an oral antibiotic as well.

> **MITES**
> If your cat has coffee grounds–type particles in her ear, she most likely has ear mites. If any of your pets get ear mites, you need to treat all of your animals.

falls

POTENTIALLY FATAL? YES

Believe it or not, more than a few vets will tell you that cats actually have a better chance of surviving a fall from 10 stories than from five stories. A falling cat will continue to accelerate until she reaches terminal velocity at 60 miles per hour. As long as a falling cat is accelerating, her body will remain tense and she will be unable to turn herself right side up. Once a cat reaches terminal velocity (at about five stories), she is able to turn right side up, at which point she relaxes her muscles and spreads out her body. This not only softens the impact, but also slows her fall speed, both of which decrease the chances of injury and death.

> *Righting reflex describes a cat's ability to land on her feet. In addition to being extremely agile, cats also have the ability to orient themselves spatially through an organ in their inner ear, which allows them to turn themselves right-side up in the air. Cats cannot fully rely on this reflex until seven weeks of age.*
>
> *High-rise syndrome is a term vets use to describe the direct correlation between the growing number of cats injured in falls and the increase in the number of high-rise apartment buildings.*

PREVENTABLE? YES

- Do not open second-story (and higher) windows — even a little bit — unless they are securely screened and you are certain the screen will withstand the weight of your cat.
- Do not permit your cat to go onto second-story decks or balconies.

TREATABLE? TO AN EXTENT

If your cat falls from the second or higher story of a building, get her checked out by your vet or animal emergency facility as soon as possible.

- Your cat may also have sustained any number of internal injuries that you cannot see.
- She may have broken bones and/or her hard palate.
- Her teeth may have been knocked out.

feline cognitive dysfunction (FCD)

Cats lose some cognitive ability as they age, and sooner or later most cats will exhibit one or two of the symptoms of FCD. These behaviors are not a normal part of the aging process, however. If your cat exhibits more than a couple of these symptoms, and your vet has ruled out other causes, you should get your cat checked for FCD.

SIGNS OF FCD
- Confusion
- Change in behavior patterns and attitude
- Change in sleep patterns
- Soiling outside the litter box

TREATABLE? **TO AN EXTENT**
While there is no cure for FCD, symptoms are treatable with a medication called Anipryl®, which increases the amount of dopamine going to the brain while decreasing the production of free radicals. Like most medications, Anipryl® is not without its side effects, so carefully weigh the pros and cons with your veterinarian before starting your cat on this medication.

Notes

when to see your vet

Unfortunately, despite preventive measures, older cats are more prone to illness and disease. If your cat has any of the following symptoms, schedule an appointment with your vet as soon as possible. These symptoms are not a normal result of the aging process.

- Abnormal swelling or lumps
- Sores that don't heal
- Eye discharge
- Nasal discharge
- Bleeding or discharge from any body opening
- Stiffness or lameness
- Diarrhea or vomiting that lasts longer than a day
- Difficulty defecating
- Difficulty urinating
- Increased urination and/or change in urine color
- Inappropriate elimination and/or spraying
- Refusal to use a clean litter box
- Difficulty breathing
- Excessive panting

- Difficulty eating or swallowing
- Loss of appetite
- Weight loss
- Increased thirst/water intake
- Difficulty or reluctance to do routine activities
- Exhaustion and/or apathy
- Sudden change in activity level
- Unusual aggression
- Change in sleep patterns
- Confusion
- Excessive grooming
- Offensive body odor
- Offensive breath
- Offensive ear odor or dirty ears
- Overgrown and/or brittle claws
- Poor coat condition
  - Bald spots
  - Dull in appearance
  - Mats
  - Excessive shedding

For information on specific conditions, diseases, and illnesses, see specific topics in this section.

VET CONTACT INFORMATION

☐ Business card in plastic pocket

Veterinarian name . . . .

Phone (. . . .) . . . . — . . . .

Address . . . .

Closest cross street . . . .

City, state, ZIP . . . .

. . . .

Office hours

Weekdays . . . . — . . . . 24/7 ☐

feline immunodeficiency virus (FIV)

FIV is a slow-acting disease that suppresses the immune system in cats. FIV has been compared to — but does not cause — HIV in humans. Cats most commonly become infected with FIV from being bitten by another cat with the disease. As a result, strays and unaltered males with access to the outdoors are most at risk for catching this disease.

SIGNS OF FIV

- Chronic bladder infections
- Diarrhea
- Weight loss
- Chronic respiratory infections
- Eye infections
- Skin infections and worsening of the overall condition of the coat
- Inflammation of the gums
- Secondary viral and bacterial infections
- Seizures
- Fever
- Change in behavior

TRANSMISSIBLE TO HUMANS? NO

POTENTIALLY FATAL? YES

FIV will not directly kill a cat. However, the disease leaves the cat more susceptible to, and unable to fight off, secondary infections.

PREVENTABLE? YES

- Keep your cat indoors.
- Neuter your male cat if he has access to the outdoors.
- Never bring another cat (or kitten) into your home unless you are certain the cat is current on vaccinations and does not have any infections or viruses.
- Anytime you come into contact with a cat that may be infected with FIV (kittens, outdoor cats, and strays are the most likely to contract this virus), always wash your hands and clothing before touching your cat or anything she may touch.
- Do not let your cat share food dishes or litter boxes with an infected or potentially infected cat.

You can get your cat a vaccination for FIV. But while it reduces your cat's chances of becoming infected with FIV, it is not 100 percent effective. For more information about this vaccination, see page 39 in CAT CONCERNS & CARE.

CARING FOR AN FIV-POSITIVE CAT

There is no cure for FIV. With proper veterinary care and a nutritious diet, however, you can manage the disease.

- Keep your cat indoors and away from other cats at all times. This not only protects uninfected cats from being exposed to FIV, but also prevents FIV-positive cats from catching any illnesses other cats may be carrying.
- Take your cat for a checkup twice a year.
- Take your cat to the vet immediately if you notice any changes in her health.
- Do not feed raw and/or unpasteurized food to your cat.

feline infectious peritonitis (FIP)

FIP is an infection caused by the coronavirus. Most cats exposed to FIP make a full recovery. Some cats, though, develop one or both of the two lethal forms of the disease, effusive FIP and noneffusive FIP. Cats that live in groups (shelters, catteries) are most at risk for FIP exposure. Not all cats that are exposed to FIP become infected; kittens, older cats, and cats with compromised and/or weakened immune systems are most susceptible.

FIP is most commonly spread from cat to cat through direct contact, but it can also be transmitted through litter boxes, feeding dishes, and any other item an infected cat uses. The virus remains active for weeks on contaminated surfaces; it is quickly neutralized with cleaning products and disinfectants.

SIGNS OF FIP EXPOSURE

Some of the signs of FIP are very mild and hard to distinguish:

- Intestinal problems
- Malaise
- Runny nose
- Sneezing
- Watery eyes

SIGNS OF LETHAL FIP INFECTION

Effusive (wet) FIP

- Difficulty breathing
- Fluid buildup in the abdomen and/or chest
- Malaise
- Worsening of the overall condition of the coat
- Weight loss

Noneffusive (dry) FIP

- Eye infections
- Fever
- Anemia
- Jaundice
- Increased thirst
- Increased urination
- Diarrhea
- Vomiting
- Weight loss
- Change in attitude/behavior
- Malaise
- Neurological problems
- Seizures

TRANSMISSIBLE TO HUMANS? **NO**

POTENTIALLY FATAL? **YES**

The incubation period between exposure and full-blown infection can last from weeks to years, depending on which form of lethal FIP infection is contracted.

- The life expectancy of a cat that exhibits clinical signs of effusive FIP ranges from days to weeks.
- The life expectancy of a cat exhibiting the clinical signs of noneffusive FIP ranges from weeks to months.

PREVENTABLE? **YES**

- Keep your cat's vaccinations up to date.
- Do not allow other cats (or kittens) in your home unless you are certain they do not have FIP.
- Talk to your vet about whether your cat should be given the FIP vaccination. (It is not 100 percent effective in protecting cats from FIP.)
- Anytime you come into contact with a cat that may be infectious (outdoor cats, strays, and kittens are most at risk for contracting the disease), always wash your hands and clothing before touching your cat or anything she may touch.

CARING FOR A CAT WITH FIP

There is no cure or effective treatment for FIP. Once a cat has been diagnosed with FIP, veterinary care usually shifts from treatment to making a cat as comfortable as possible by managing pain and symptoms.

feline leukemia virus (FeLV)

FeLV has also been compared to HIV in humans, but it does not cause HIV. In addition to damaging the body's immune system, making it difficult for the body to fight off infection, FeLV frequently causes cancer and blood-related diseases in cats.

FeLV is most commonly spread from cat to cat through bite wounds or from mother to kitten in utero and through nursing. However, it can also be transmitted through litter boxes, feeding dishes, and mutual grooming.

Strays and unaltered males with access to the outdoors are most at risk for becoming exposed to FeLV, but not all cats that are exposed to FeLV become infected. Kittens and cats with weakened and/or compromised immune systems are the most susceptible to the virus.

SIGNS OF FeLV
- Chronic bladder infections
- Chronic diarrhea
- Loss of appetite
- Weight loss
- Chronic respiratory infections
- Eye infections and ulcers
- Skin infections and worsening of the overall condition of the coat
- Inflammation of the gums and/or mouth
- Secondary viral and bacterial infections
- Seizures
- Swollen lymph nodes
- Change in behavior

TRANSMISSIBLE TO HUMANS? **NO**

POTENTIALLY FATAL? **YES**

The life expectancy for a cat infected with FeLV ranges from several months to several years.

PREVENTABLE? **YES**
- Keep your cat indoors.
- Never bring another cat (or kitten) into your home unless you are certain the cat does not have FeLV.
- Neuter your male cat and keep him indoors.
- Anytime you come into contact with a cat that may be infected with FeLV (kittens, outdoor cats, and strays are the most likely to contract this virus), always wash your hands and clothing before touching your cat or anything she may touch.
- Do not let your cat share food dishes or litter boxes with an infected or potentially infected cat.

If you absolutely must permit your cat access to the outdoors, have her vaccinated. But be aware that while this vaccination does reduce your cat's chances of becoming infected with FeLV, it is not 100 percent effective. For more information on this vaccination, see page 40 in **CAT CONCERNS & CARE**.

CARING FOR AN FeLV-POSITIVE CAT

There is no cure for FeLV. With proper veterinary care and a nutritious diet, however, the disease can be managed.

- Keep your cat indoors and away from other cats at all times. This not only protects uninfected cats from being exposed to FeLV but also prevents FeLV-positive cats from catching any illnesses other cats may be carrying.
- Take your cat for a checkup twice a year.
- Take your cat to the vet immediately if you notice any changes in her health.
- Do not feed raw and/or unpasteurized food to your cat.

feline lower urinary tract disease (FLUTD)

A common affliction in cats, FLUTD is a general term for any sort of bladder and/or urethra infection. There are two types of FLUTDs: nonobstructive, which is much more common and not quite as serious, and obstructive, which means there are crystals or stones in the bladder that can create blockages.

SIGNS OF FLUTD

- Blood in urine
- Frequent (often unsuccessful) attempts to urinate
- Licking the genital area
- Straining and/or in pain when urinating
- Urinating outside the litter box

POTENTIALLY FATAL? YES

PREVENTABLE? TO AN EXTENT

- Always make sure your cat has plenty of water.
- Switch your cat to a wet-food diet. (Wet foods contain significantly more water than dry foods.)
- Eliminate or reduce stress. (Introducing a new pet to the household, for example, can be particularly stressful for some cats, especially if the animals do not get along.)
- Any time you change your cat's diet, do so very gradually, slowly mixing in more and more of the new food with the old food, until you have completely phased out the old food.

TREATABLE? YES

Nonobstructive FLUTD usually resolves itself on its own within a matter of days. Obstructive FLUTD is much more serious and can be life-threatening. Only a vet can tell whether your cat has obstructive or nonobstructive FLUTD. So if your cat exhibits any of the signs for this disease, to be on the safe side you should get to your vet or animal emergency facility as soon as possible.

Depending on the size and type of the crystals/stones, your vet may recommend any of the following treatments for obstructive FLUTD:

- A diet that will dissolve the stones
- Surgery to remove the stones
- Removing the blockage by pushing the crystals/stones back into the bladder with a catheter.

fleabites

In addition to making all members (animal and human) of your home absolutely miserable with fleabites, fleas, left untreated, can cause numerous problems:

- The most aggravating but least serious condition fleas cause is skin problems, which include hair loss from excessive scratching, as well as scabs and bumps.
- Fleas cause anemia, which may cause death in kittens and older or sick cats.
- Fleas carry tapeworm, which can be life-threatening.
- Fleas carry the plague, which is unquestionably deadly.

frostbite

SIGNS OF FROSTBITE
- Blisters on the affected area
- Ice on the body and limbs
- Shivering
- Skin that changes color from bright red to very pale when warmed, and then eventually to black

POTENTIALLY FATAL? NO
Frostbite is not fatal. In extreme cases, however, limbs may need to be amputated.

PREVENTABLE? YES
- Do not leave your cat outdoors — or let her outdoors — in freezing weather.

TREATABLE? YES
Take your cat to the vet or animal emergency facility to be treated ASAP.

If for whatever reason, you are unable to get to the vet, perform the following procedures. You will still need to get your cat checked out as soon as possible, because it does not take much for frostbitten skin to become infected.

- Heat the affected area with warm — not hot! — water.
- Gently pat dry to the affected area — do not rub it!

- Put a Vaseline-based ointment on the affected area. Then wrap your cat in a warm, dry towel. (Put the towel in the dryer for a minute or two first.)
- Offer your cat warm sugar water (2 tablespoons of sugar to 1 cup of water).

> **WARNING!**
> Use extreme caution as you warm up your cat.
> - It may sting, and your cat may attempt to bite and/or scratch you!
> - You don't want to burn your cat.

CATS MOST AT RISK
- Cats that are left outdoors in freezing weather, particularly kittens and sick, injured, and/or older cats.

BODY PARTS MOST SUSCEPTIBLE TO FROSTBITE
- Ear tips
- Face
- Paw pads
- Scrotum
- Tail

DON'TS OF TREATING FROSTBITE

DON'T rub the affected area. Doing so can loosen toxins within the tissue and cause further damage.

DON'T apply snow or ice.

DON'T submerge your cat in warm water. Doing so may cause hypothermia.

DON'T warm up your cat too fast. Rapid heating can be painful.

DON'T let your cat bite at or scratch the affected area.

heartworm disease

Heartworms are not nearly as common in cats as they are in dogs. When cats do get heartworm disease, however, it is very serious and not easily treatable, so it is a good idea to take preventive measures.

Heartworm eggs are transmitted to cats when infected mosquitoes bite them. Indoor cats are protected only to the degree that you are able to prevent mosquitoes from entering your home.

SIGNS OF HEARTWORM DISEASE
- Choking
- Chronic cough
- Difficulty breathing
- Shortness of breath
- Vomiting/gagging
- Weight loss
- Weakness
- Fainting
- Seizures
- Blindness
- Sudden death

It is possible for a cat infected with heartworms to exhibit none of the clinical signs.

TRANSMISSIBLE TO HUMANS? NO

POTENTIALLY FATAL? YES

PREVENTABLE? YES
- Consistently administer heartworm medication if your cat is at risk.
- Do everything you can to eliminate your cat's exposure to mosquitoes.
- Keep your cat indoors.

TREATABLE? TO A SMALL EXTENT
Unfortunately, there is no easy cure for heartworm disease in cats. The medication used to treat heartworm in dogs is toxic to cats. Additionally, dead heartworms in cats pose a serious health risk, because they can block blood vessels. In severe cases, the heartworms can be surgically removed. Most often, however, vets prefer to monitor the cat, at six-month intervals, to see if the cat will recover without medical intervention, while treating respiratory symptoms with prednisone.

Unlike in dogs, where starting heartworm prevention can be harmful to a dog with heartworm disease, preventive medication is recommended for cats with the disease.

heatstroke

SIGNS OF HEATSTROKE
- Apathy
- Dizziness
- Weakness
- Exhaustion
- Shallow/labored/noisy breathing
- Fever of 104° or higher
- Diarrhea
- Vomiting
- Glazed eyes
- Red or pale gums
- Salivating
- Shock
- Coma

POTENTIALLY FATAL? YES

PREVENTABLE? YES
- Always check to make sure your cat hasn't snuck into your dryer before starting it.
- Make sure your cat is not able to sneak into and get trapped in enclosed spaces such as cars, car trunks, sheds, etc.

HEATSTROKE

Do not cool down your cat too quickly. Doing so can cause hypothermia. Cool her down to 103° to 104°, then transport her to the vet immediately. Make sure to keep her cool and out of the sun while traveling to the vet.

- Normal body temperature: 100.5°–102.5°
- Moderate heatstroke: 103°–106°
- Severe heatstroke: 106° and higher

If your cat has a fever of 106° or higher, she is in critical condition and needs to be taken to an animal emergency room immediately.

- Never leave your cat alone inside the car. Even on mild days, the temperature inside the car can rise to dangerous levels. Cracking windows does not provide sufficient ventilation.
- Make sure your cat always has plenty of water.
- Never leave your cat outside or confined to a crate in the heat.
- If your cat absolutely must stay outside, make sure she has access to shelter from the sun.

CATS MOST AT RISK:

- Cats with heart conditions
- Cats with respiratory conditions
- Long-haired cats
- Older cats
- Overweight cats
- Kittens
- Short-nosed cats

TREATABLE? YES

Follow these steps to cool your cat and then get her to your vet or animal emergency facility immediately!

- Stop all activity immediately.
- Remove your cat from the heat immediately.
- Soak, rinse, or wet your cat with cool — not cold — water.
- Place a wet towel around your cat's neck. (Do not cover her entire body.)
- Place a disposable ice pack (or a bag of frozen corn or peas) on her head.
- Offer a small amount of room-temperature water.

Notes

homeopathy

Homeopathy is an alternative approach to medicine. In homeopathic treatment, medication that exacerbates preexisting symptoms of illness is administered to induce the body to heal itself. The objective in homeopathy is to cure the underlying illness completely, rather than manage the symptoms through medication.

hookworms

Cats get hookworms from walking on soil, grass, or beaches that are infested with hookworm larvae. They can pass it onto their kittens through the placenta and through their milk. The larvae burrow into the cat's skin. Once inside the cat, they journey to the intestine, where they mature.

SIGNS OF HOOKWORMS
- Anemia
- Unexplained exhaustion
- Weight loss
- Bloody diarrhea
- Pale gums
- Skin irritation
- Thinning coat
- Stunted growth in kittens

TRANSMISSIBLE TO HUMANS? YES
The larvae can burrow into your skin and cause "ground itch," but hookworms do not mature in people.

PREVENTABLE? YES
- Regularly clean your cat's litter box.
- Always wear gloves and wash your hands with soapy, hot water when you are finished cleaning the litter box.
- Always wear shoes when walking in damp soil or soil that may contain dog or cat waste.
- Promptly deworm your infected pet(s).

TREATABLE? YES
It is necessary to administer injections or oral tablets twice over a monthlong period. The medication works only on adult hookworms, not larvae.

CATS MOST LIKELY TO GET HOOKWORM
Kittens

POTENTIALLY FATAL? YES

hypothermia

SIGNS OF HYPOTHERMIA
- Dilated pupils
- Shallow and/or slow breathing
- Shivering
- Stiffness
- Apathy
- Weakness
- Coma

PREVENTABLE? YES
- Never leave your cat outdoors in cold or inclement weather.
- Never leave your cat in the car in cold or inclement weather.
- Make sure your cat is not able to sneak into and get trapped in your refrigerator or freezer. Storage freezers that are not opened frequently pose the greatest danger.
- If your cat absolutely must stay outside, make sure she has access to shelter from the cold.

TREATABLE? YES
- Contact your vet for advice ASAP. You may need to take your cat to the vet for treatment.
- Wrap your cat in a warm, dry towel. (Put the towel in the dryer for a minute or two first.)
- Use your body heat to warm your cat by wrapping yourself up in a blanket with her.

- Apply the following under your cat's armpits or abdomen (wherever your cat has the least amount of fur):
    - Water bottle with warm — not hot! — water. If you don't have a water bottle, a plastic soda bottle will work, but be sure to insulate the bottle with a blanket or towel so you don't burn your cat.
    - Well-insulated heating pad set on warm — not hot!
    - Hair dryer set on low, with warm — not hot! — air.

> **WARNING!**
> Use extreme caution so you don't burn your cat! It's a good idea to place a finger or two between your cat and the water bottle or heating pad to help ensure that your cat does not get burned.

- If your cat is already wet, you may want to put her in a warm — not hot! — bath. (Speak to your vet before immersing your cat's body in water. If your vet needs to see your cat, it is not a good idea to get her any wetter than she is. If you do immerse your cat in warm water, be extremely careful not to get scratched and/or bitten.)
- Offer your cat warm sugar water (2 tablespoons sugar to 1 cup of water).

CATS AT MOST RISK FOR GETTING HYPOTHERMIA
- Cats with access to the outdoors — particularly cats with no access to shelter
- Short-haired cats
- Wet cats
- Kittens
- Older cats
- Injured and/or sick cats

> **HYPOTHERMIA**
> - Normal body temperature: 100.5°–102.5°
> - Mild hypothermia: 96°–100°
> - Moderate hypothermia: 90°–95°
> - Severe hypothermia: 90° or below

incontinence

> See **SOILING OUTSIDE THE LITTER BOX (CHAPTER 2)** *for more information.*

Notes . . . .

. . . .

. . . .

. . . .

. . . .

lyme disease

While there have been documented cases of Lyme disease in all 50 states and Canada, it is most prevalent in New England and the mid-Atlantic states. Although Lyme disease is more commonly associated with dogs, cats are not immune to it.

Cats with access to the outdoors, especially wooded areas or areas with tall grass, are most at risk for catching this disease. However, indoor cats that share their environment with animals that have access to the outdoors, especially areas where the tick population might be high, are also at risk. Indoor cats are protected from Lyme disease only to the degree that you are able to prevent infected ticks from being carried into your home — on the body of a person or dog.

SIGNS OF LYME DISEASE

- Severe joint pain
- Swelling in nodes
- Limping
- Apathy
- Loss of appetite
- Temperature of 103° or higher

TRANSMISSIBLE TO HUMANS? YES

POTENTIALLY FATAL? NO

Lyme disease is not fatal. The disease is debilitating, however.

PREVENTABLE? YES

- Keep your cat indoors. (This is probably the single best way to prevent your cat from contracting Lyme disease.)

- Always wear long sleeves and pants in the woods and tall grass, and give yourself a full-body tick check when you return, to ensure that you don't bring ticks into the house.

- If your cat does have access to the outdoors, give her a full-body tick check every 24 hours.

- If any of your pets have access to the outdoors, use a flea- and tick-preventive treatment on all of your animals, even if you keep your cat indoors. (Still do full-body tick checks on them after they have been in the woods or tall grass, though, as they can still carry ticks into the house, where they can attach to your cat.)

- Spray your lawn with vet-approved tick killer.

- Keep your lawn mowed.

TREATABLE? YES

Your vet will most likely prescribe tetracycline. With timely treatment, most cats make a full recovery with no permanent joint or nerve damage.

> It usually takes at least 24 hours for a tick to transmit Lyme disease. By doing a daily full-body tick check on your cat and any other pets, you seriously reduce their chances of catching this disease. For information on how to remove a tick, see **TICKS** on page 95 in this section.

panting

Cats pant to cool themselves off. However, if you notice your cat panting excessively and/or over a prolonged period of time, check for underlying causes (such as heatstroke, shock, or trauma) and consult your vet as soon as possible. For more information on heatstroke and shock, see specific topics in this section.

poisons

You can reach the ASPCA Animal Poison Control Center at (888) 426-4435.

A veterinary toxicologist is on duty 24 hours a day, 365 days a year, to diagnose your pet and recommend the appropriate treatment.

There is a $50 consultation fee, which includes unlimited follow-up phone calls. The veterinary toxicologist will also advise your veterinarian at no additional charge.

To have the consultation fee automatically added to your phone bill, call (900) 433-0000. Do not dial the 900 number for follow-up phone calls. Instead, call (888) 426-4435.

> ### WARNING!
> If you suspect that your cat has been poisioned, call your vet or the ASPCA Animal poision Control Center immediately at (888) 426-4435. (See **POISONS** on this page for information on the consultation fee, as well as page 88 for a list of items that are toxic to your pet.)

Notes

**COMMON HOUSEHOLD PRODUCTS
THAT ARE TOXIC TO YOUR CAT***

Alcohol
Ant & roach traps/spray
Antifreeze
Avocado
Candy
Chocolate
Citronella candles
Coffee
Flea foggers/bombs/powder
Fruit pits and seeds
Gardening fertilizer
Garlic
Grapes
Ibuprofen
Ice-melting salts
Insecticide
Lead (paint)
Medications (human)
Mold
Mothballs
Mushrooms
Mustard seeds
Nicotine
Macadamia nuts
Onions/onion powder
Plants (not all; see box)
Potpourri/liquid potpourri
Raisins
Rat poison
Salt
Swimming pool chemicals
Tea
Vitamins
Walnuts
Zinc (in pennies)

*Do not assume that something is not toxic
simply because it is not on this list.

PLANTS

*It is a fact of life that many cats like to eat
or at least chew on plants. While many
household plants are nontoxic to cats, many
are not safe to have around at all. Also keep
in mind that some varieties of the same spe-
cies may be fine and others not. For example, many but not all ferns are nontoxic.*

**THE TEN MOST TOXIC PLANTS
(ACCORDING TO THE ASPCA)**

*Azalea/rhododendron
Castor bean
Cyclamen
Kalanchoe
Lily
Marijuana
Oleander
Sago
Tulip/narcissus bulbs
Yew*

**POPULAR HOUSE PLANTS
THAT ARE NONTOXIC**

*African violet (red)
Begonia
Bird of paradise
Gardenia
Jade plant
Orchid
Spider plant
Venus flytrap*

 *This is not a comprehensive list. For
a complete list of toxic and nontoxic
plants, visit the ASPCA Web site at
www.aspca.org.*

puncture wounds

POTENTIALLY FATAL? YES

With sharp teeth and even sharper claws, cats can inflict deep puncture wounds in one another. These wounds are problematic in that they are not always easy to spot, and they are highly prone to infection. If the wound does not get filled with bacteria when the injury occurs, it almost certainly will when the cat licks her wound, covering the cut in bacteria-filled saliva. When the body attempts to fight the infection, pus surrounds the wound, creating an abscess (see box on p. 90). Proper cleaning and treatment of wounds is essential.

SIGNS YOUR CAT MAY HAVE A PUNCTURE WOUND

- Heat around a particular body part
- Excessive licking on a particular body part
- Lump
- Tenderness in a particular body part
- Limping

If your cat has no visible injuries but is showing signs of shock, she may have an internal puncture wound. Take your cat to the vet or an animal emergency facility immediately!

TREATABLE? YES

- Stop the bleeding by applying continuous pressure to the wound with a sterile bandage.
- If possible, elevate the wound while you continue applying pressure.
- Do not apply a tourniquet!
- For minor scratches, you may be able to treat the wound at home. But always contact your vet to make sure you don't need to take your cat for treatment.
  - Put on a pair of disposable gloves.
  - Clean the wound using 3 percent hydrogen peroxide solution (the standard drugstore variety).
  - Carefully — and gently — remove any debris or foreign objects from the surface of the wound.
  - Follow up with antibiotic ointment two times a day and watch for signs of infection.
  - Do not remove anything that is lodged in the wound — doing so could cause your cat serious harm. If you see something inside the wound, take her to the vet ASAP.

- For more serious wounds, take your cat to the vet ASAP so that your vet may provide the appropriate treatment, which may include cleaning and treating the wound, prescribing oral and/or topical antibiotics, and/or giving your cat an antibiotic in shot form.

> If your cat attempts to claw at or chew on the wound, try spraying a little Bitter Apple on the bandage or put an Elizabethan collar on your cat. Do not apply Bitter Apple directly on the wound.

CATS MOST AT RISK FOR GETTING PUNCTURE WOUNDS

Cats with access to the outdoors, especially unaltered male cats, since they are the most likely to get into fights.

ABSCESSES

The way to prevent abscesses is to prevent infection, by cleaning and treating puncture wounds immediately. Unfortunately, you cannot treat a wound you cannot see, and puncture wounds, particularly scratch wounds, often go undetected until an abscess has already formed.

If you suspect that your cat has an abscess, take her to your vet or animal emergency facility ASAP — definitely that day. Treating an abscess usually requires surgery under anesthesia so your vet can drain the pus from the wound and then remove all dead and infected tissue. Your cat may require a few days of post-op care at the vet's before being discharged. Once your cat is discharged, your vet will provide you with the necessary instructions, medications, and ointments. Keep a close eye on the wound. If it looks like another abscess is forming, or the wound is not healing properly, take your cat in for a follow-up visit ASAP.

If left untreated, abscesses can be fatal, sometimes causing death quite quickly, other times shortening a cat's lifespan.

SIGNS OF AN ABSCESS
- Fever
- Heat around the wound
- Lump around the wound
- Tenderness around the wound
- Loss of appetite
- Sleeping more than usual

ringworms

Despite its name, ringworm actually has nothing to do with worms. It's a fungus that takes the shape of a puffy ring on infected people and animals.

Ringworm is highly contagious. Cats can catch it from, and give it to, people, other cats, dogs, and rodents. Ringworm is transmitted through direct contact as well as by touching contaminated surfaces, including floors, countertops, beds, blankets, sheets, towels, and so on.

SIGNS OF RINGWORM
- Signature puffy, ring-shaped lesion
- Circular patches of hair loss
- Scaly, gray patches on skin

TRANSMISSIBLE TO HUMANS? **YES! VERY!**
Children are particularly susceptible to ringworm. If infection does spread to your family, get prescription topical cream ASAP. Be vigilant about washing used towels, linens, and clothing as often as possible until the infection is cleared up.

The following measures are helpful — but not foolproof — in stopping your cat (or other animal) from transmitting ringworm to your entire household.

- Keep the infected animal confined to one easy-to-clean room until the fungus is completely gone. (Keep all children and uninfected household pets out of this room and away from the infected cat.)
- Always wash your hands and clothing after touching the infected cat and/or anything she may have come into contact with.
- Thoroughly disinfect any surfaces and wash any linens the infected cat has come into contact with.

POTENTIALLY FATAL? **NO**

PREVENTABLE? **YES**

- Keep your cat indoors.
- Do not allow other cats (or kittens) into your home unless you are certain they do not have ringworm.
- Do not pet or touch kittens (unless you are certain they do not have ringworm) or strays.

TREATABLE? **YES**

- Antifungal shampoo
- Topical antifungal medication
- Griseofulvin tablets (prescription)
- Lime sulfur dips

 In some instances, your vet may recommend shaving the hair around the infection or shaving the entire body to prevent the ringworm from spreading and to promote healing.

roundworms

Roundworms are parasitic worms that live in the small intestines. Cats get roundworms from eating the feces of infected animals, including other cats, dogs, chickens, and rodents, and from eating cockroaches and earthworms. Kittens can also get roundworms from their mother's placenta (before birth) and from nursing.

SIGNS OF ROUNDWORMS

- Diarrhea
- Vomiting
- Loss of appetite
- Pot-bellied appearance
- Weight loss

TRANSMISSIBLE TO HUMANS? **YES**

Roundworm eggs, which are shed in cat feces, cause a whole slew of serious problems in humans if they are ingested. So if you didn't already have enough reasons to keep your toddler out of the litter box, the possibility of roundworm infection is another. In addition, make sure toddlers stay out of soil or sand that may be contaminated. Except in Third World countries, roundworms are rarely transmitted to adults.

POTENTIALLY FATAL? **NO**

PREVENTABLE? **YES**

- Clean litter boxes daily.
- Promptly deworm any infected cat or other pet in the household.

TREATMENT

Your vet will prescribe oral medication.

shock

SIGNS YOUR CAT IS IN SHOCK

- Agitation
- Cold paws
- Curled tongue
- Pale gums
- Panting
- Rapid or irregular breathing
- Rapid or irregular heartbeat
- Subnormal temperature
- Poor balance; unsteadiness
- Loss of consciousness

POTENTIALLY FATAL? **YES**

PREVENTABLE? **TO AN EXTENT**

Shock stems from trauma, illness, or infection as well as hypothermia and heat stroke. By taking measures to prevent or minimize your cat's exposure to these conditions, you go a long way toward preventing shock in your cat.

TREATABLE? **YES**

If your cat is in shock, you need to get her to your vet or animal emergency facility

immediately. First, take measures to prevent the condition from worsening:

- Wrap your cat in a dry (if possible, warm) towel — unless your cat may be suffering from heatstroke.
- Apply a disposable hot-compress pack — unless your cat may be suffering from heatstroke.
- Stop any bleeding.
- If your cat is unconscious, make sure she is breathing properly and that her airway is clear. (See **CHOKING** on page 72 in this section for more information.)
- If your cat is dehydrated, feed her sugar/honey water with a dropper.

HOLISTIC REMEDIES

- Giving your cat several drops of Rescue Remedy® in her mouth will go a long way toward calming her down.
- Giving your cat several drops of arnica in her mouth will help with her physical symptoms.

> **QUICK SHOCK TEST**
> *Press on your cat's gums. If they do not return to their original color within a couple of seconds, your cat is most likely suffering from shock or dehydration.*

CAUSES OF SHOCK

- Allergic reaction
- Cat or animal bite
- Snake or toad bite
- Bee, insect, or spider sting
- Choking
- Being hit by a car
- Gunshot wound — including wounds from BB guns or air guns
- Dehydration
- Heatstroke
- Hypothermia
- Poisoning

skunks

> **WARNING!**
> If your cat has been bitten by a skunk, do not — under any circumstances — touch the open wound! Using extreme caution to avoid being scratched or bitten, secure your cat with a large towel or blanket and get your cat to the vet immediately!

Believe it or not, upon occasion cats and skunks have been known to coexist quite peacefully. They have even been found sharing a dish of food. However, rabies is very common in skunks, so you do not want your kitty making friends with them. Also, if a cat startles a skunk, or simply gets caught at the wrong place at the wrong time, the skunk will spray.

When a skunk sprays a cat, the oil often gets in the cat's eyes and stings. In an attempt to stop the burning, your cat will wipe her face against anything she can — including furniture — so think twice before giving her free run of your house until you've "deskunked" her. This oil is also impossible to get out of clothes, so change into clothes you can discard before you bathe your cat.

PREVENTABLE? YES

- Keep your cat indoors.
- Do not leave doggie doors open.
- Do not leave pet food (or any other food) outside.
- Install a fence around your property — it needs to be at least 18 inches deep to prevent skunks from digging under it.
- Install lattice or something similar to prevent skunks from setting up camp under your house.
- Make sure trashcans are securely closed.

GETTING RID OF A SKUNK

- If you find a skunk in your garage, leave a door open for it to get out and leave all of the lights on as well as a radio, tuned to a news station.

- Gently shoo it outside — but give it enough space that it doesn't feel threatened enough to spray you.

- NEVER attempt to pick up or touch a skunk — at the very least you'll get sprayed, and you may get bitten.

- Drench rags in ammonia and leave them in the skunk's favorite spot(s).

- Sprinkle mothballs in and around the skunk's favorite spot(s).

WARNING SIGNS THAT A SKUNK IS ABOUT TO SPRAY

If a skunk starts stomping its feet or bushing its tail out, make a fast retreat.

TREATABLE? **TO AN EXTENT**

DESKUNKING A CAT

- Before you worry about dealing with the odor, examine your cat to make sure she does not have any bites or scrapes. Skunks carry the rabies virus, and if your cat has been bitten, you need to get her to a veterinarian immediately. Do not touch any open wounds.

- Flush your cat's eyes with saline solution and wipe her nose with a sanitary wipe. If your cat exhibits behavior that would indicate that her eyes still sting (after you have flushed them) or if her eyes become overly red or swollen, take her to the vet ASAP!

- Treat your cat with a deskunking formula such as Nature's Miracle Skunk Odor Remover or a home remedy (see box). Treat only the part of her body that has been sprayed

— treating her whole body will only spread the oil.

HOMEMADE DESKUNKING MIXTURE
- 1 quart hydrogen peroxide (2 pints standard drugstore-variety which contains 3 percent hydrogen peroxide)
- 1/4 cup baking soda
- 1 teaspoon liquid dish soap

Directions:
1. Put rubber gloves on before you mix the ingredients.
2. Keep the mixture away from your face and your cat's face.
3. Wet your cat's fur with water, then work the mixture through her fur. Let it set for three to five minutes.
4. Rinse your cat's fur thoroughly with water.
5. Dispose of all unused mixture! (It will explode if you keep it in a sealed container.)

 This mixture will bleach your cat's fur. It is extremely abrasive, so use as little as possible.

snakebites

> **WARNING!**
> Snakebites require urgent veterinary care! Get your cat to your vet or an animal emergency facility immediately!

SIGNS YOUR CAT HAS BEEN BITTEN BY A SNAKE
- Swelling around wound
- Vomiting
- Extreme thirst
- Fever
- Numbness around mouth
- Low blood pressure
- Rapid or irregular breathing
- Rapid or irregular heartbeat
- Confusion
- Shock

POTENTIALLY FATAL? YES

PREVENTABLE? YES
- Keep your cat indoors.
- Do not leave windows or doors open. (Snakes can enter homes through doggie doors.)

TREATABLE? TO AN EXTENT
- Wrap your cat in a towel or blanket to immobilize her.
- Remain calm and do everything you can to keep your cat calm.

There is no quick cure for poisonous snakebites. Even if your vet is able to apply the appropriate antivenom in a timely manner, your cat will still require intensive care.

SNAKEBITES
Both activity and excitement cause snake venom to spread faster. Do everything you can to keep your cat still and make her feel secure.
- Only if you can do so safely (and quickly), identify the snake. Otherwise, leave it to your vet to determine the type of snakebite based on the shape of the bite and symptoms your cat exhibits.
- Transport your cat to the vet or an animal emergency facility immediately — your cat requires urgent medical attention! If possible, have someone else drive so you can tend to your cat en route.
- Only if you can do so safely, call your vet or animal emergency facility en route to alert them to the situation and your pending arrival.
- Do not wash the wound.
- Do not put ice on the wound.
- Do not cut or suck on the wound — this will not effectively remove snake venom, and it will expose you to the venom.
- Do not give pain medication.

NONVENOMOUS SNAKEBITES
The good news is that not all snakes are venomous, which means not all snakebites are poisonous. Even if the snakebite is not poisonous, however, your cat most likely has a puncture wound that a vet will need to clean and treat.

tick bites

Ticks, which live in forests and in tall grass, suck the blood of their "host" and spread disease by spreading blood from one host to the next. For information on tick-borne **LYME DISEASE**, see page 86.

PREVENTABLE? YES
- Keep your cat indoors.
- Always wear long sleeves and pants in the woods and tall grass, and give yourself a full-body tick check when you return, to ensure that you don't bring ticks into the house.
- If your cat does have access to the outdoors, give her a full-body tick check every 24 hours.
- If any of your pets have access to the outdoors, use a flea- and tick-preventive treatment on all of your animals, even if you keep your cat indoors. (Still do full-body tick checks on them after they have been in the woods or tall grass, though, as they can still carry ticks into the house, where they can attach to your cat.)
- Spray your lawn with a vet-approved tick killer.
- Keep your lawn mowed.

HOW TO REMOVE A TICK
- Separate your cat's fur so you can clearly see and reach the tick.
- Using a cotton swab, douse the tick and surrounding area in rubbing alcohol.
- With a pair of tweezers, grasp the tick as close to its head (where it is attached to the body) as possible.
- Pull firmly until the tick's entire body is removed from your cat's skin.
- Flush the tick down the toilet.

- Using a sterile cotton swab, wipe the area with an antiseptic.
- Wash your hands with soap and hot water.
- Do not squeeze so hard with the tweezers that you decapitate the tick, with its head still burrowed in your cat's skin!
- Do not try to burn the tick off!
- Do not try to smother the tick with Vaseline!

west nile virus

TRANSMISSIBLE TO HUMANS? NO
According to the Centers for Disease Control, there is no evidence that West Nile virus can be transmitted from cat to human, even if an infected cat were to bite a person.

POTENTIALLY FATAL? NOT TYPICALLY
Cats rarely get West Nile virus. There are no more than a few documented cases. If your cat does contract the virus, she will probably make a full recovery.

PREVENTABLE? TO AN EXTENT
The likelihood that your cat will get West Nile virus is remote. It's a good idea, though, to protect your cat from this and other diseases by taking measures to minimize your cat's exposure to mosquitoes. The best way to do this is to keep your cat indoors.

TREATABLE? NO
Even though there's no treatment for West Nile, you can treat the symptoms with the sort of basic flu-therapy remedies you would use on a person: fluids, pain medication, and rest.

Notes

Chapter 4

 CAT TRAVEL

Instead of leaving your cat at home or boarding her while you travel, consider a third choice: bringing her with you. Many aircraft carriers allow one or two pets to fly with each passenger. If you prefer not to fly, check our list of things you can do to make your cat comfortable on a road trip. This section explores different travel options and lists a number of cat-friendly hotel chains.

in this chapter

- TRAVEL PREP
- WHAT TO PACK
- ROADTRIP TIPS
- FLYING TIPS
- GENERAL AIRLINE RULES
- AIRLINE INFORMATION AND PET POLICIES
- CAR RENTAL AGENCIES/TRAIN POLICIES
- HOTEL DO'S AND DON'TS
- CAT-FRIENDLY HOTEL CHAINS
- YOUR LIST OF PLACES TO STAY

travel prep

Before you take your cat on the family vacation, think seriously about whether she may be happier at home. Cats are creatures of habit. They don't like change, and they're really not big fans of riding in cars.

DOS AND DON'TS BEFORE YOU LEAVE

DO Confirm that your cat is welcome at your destination.

DO Schedule a checkup for your cat and have your vet issue a health certificate and a copy of her vaccination records.

DO Talk to your vet about prescribing a tranquilizer, just in case your cat has a meltdown in the car.

DO Trim your pet's claws so they don't catch on anything.

DON'T Bring your cat if she is sick or injured.

DON'T Bring your cat if she's going to be stuck alone in a hotel room the entire time.

---

what to pack

- **CAT FOOD** At a minimum, bring enough food for the first 48 hours. Unless you are certain you can get your cat's normal food at your destination, bring enough for the whole trip.
- **WATER** Bring a gallon of water from home (or purchase filtered water) to mix with the water at your destination to help prevent stomach upset. If your cat has a sensitive stomach, you may want to provide your cat with water from home or filtered water the entire time.
- **BED OR BLANKET** Many of the nicer hotels now provide beds for pets. However, bringing your cat's bed or blanket from home (with all of its familiar scents) will give your kitty an added sense of security.
- **WATER BOWL** Depending on how long you will be in the car, it's a good idea to bring a bowl with a resealable lid so you can offer your cat water on your journey.
- **DISPOSABLE LITTER BOX** Depending on how long you will be gone, you may want to bring one or more disposable litter boxes. Don't forget to bring a scooper.
- **FOOD BOWL**
- **SUNSCREEN** If your cat is going to be exposed to the sun, sunscreen is essential. The Animal Poison Control Center says any sunscreen product that is not labeled specifically for use on animals should not be used. Human sunscreen can contain zinc, salicylate and PABAs, all of which can be toxic to a cat. Sunscreen made specifically for cats is available. Check with your local pet store or visit online pet-vendors.
- **SUPPLEMENTS**
- **TREATS**
- **MEDICATIONS**
- **FIRST-AID KIT** (For information on what to put in your **FIRST-AID KIT**, see page 16.)

roadtrip tips

- Take your cat out of the carrier and let her roam around the car for a few minutes each time you stop for gas. Make sure all passengers know not to open the doors while your cat is loose.
- If you have to let your cat out of the carrier, always make sure she is securely back inside before you open any car doors.
- Give your cat access to water and a litter box when you stop, even though most cats will prefer to wait until you arrive at your destination and are away from the car.

ROADTRIP TIP

Never leave your cat in the car unattended, especially in hot or cold weather!

By leaving your cat alone in the car, you are exposing her to the following risks:

- heat stroke in hot weather
- hypothermia in cold weather
- theft

---

flying tips

Most cats meet the weight requirements to fly in the cabin, under your seat. While this unquestionably limits you from bringing much else onboard in the way of carry-on luggage, it is infinitely safer for your cat to travel in the cabin, rather than in the cargo hold.

PETS AS CARRY-ON

Most airlines allow two carry-on pets per coach passenger and one pet per first-class passenger. There is limited space for pets on each flight, however, and space is available on a first-come, first-served basis.

PETS AS CARGO

If, for whatever reason, you have to ship your cat in the cargo hold, taking the following precautions can help keep your cat safe during the trip.

- Book a direct nonstop flight:
  - during the day in cold weather
  - at night in warm weather
  - during off-peak travel times (avoid holidays and weekends)
- Travel on the same flight as your cat.
- Reconfirm your cat's reservation 24 to 48 hours before your departure. Verify that temperatures are within acceptable ranges for your cat to fly.
- Offer your cat food and water within four hours of your arrival at the airport. (Airport officials will have you confirm this in writing at check-in.)
- Before you board the plane, have a gate attendant confirm that your cat was loaded onto the plane.
- Be proactive. If you encounter delays or changes, insist that airline personnel check on your cat.
- Carry a current photograph of your pet and a description of the crate (brand, size, color, etc.).

general airline rules

In order to take your cat on the plane (whether in the cabin or cargo), you must show proof of vaccinations and present a health certificate issued no more than 10 days prior to your travel date for all legs of the trip. If you will be traveling for more than 10 days, review airline policies before making final arrangements. Your cat must be at least eight weeks old.

Make sure your cat carrier is airline approved.

THE CARRIER MUST BE:
- Sturdy
- Leakproof
- Ventilated

It must contain:
- A hinged or sliding door
- Grips or handles for lifting
- A locking device (if it has wheels)
- Two dishes for food and water — accessible from outside the carrier.

BE SURE TO:
- Place absorbent bedding a towel or blanket, inside the carrier.
- Label the carrier with your pet's name, your contact information, and your cat's final destination.
- Attach feeding instructions, to cover a 24-hour period, to the carrier.
- Display a "Live Animals" label, with letters at least one-inch high, on the top and on at least one side of the carrier.
- Label the carrier "This End Up" on at least two sides.

YOUR CAT MUST:
- Be able to stand and sit upright without her head touching the top of the carrier, and be able to turn around and lie down comfortably.
- Not be able to fit any part of her body (nose, paws, tail) through the slats in the carrier.

Notes

airline information and pet policies

> *All weight limits include the combined weight of the cat and carrier/kennel.*

AMERICAN AIRLINES
(800) 433-7300
aa.com

IN-CABIN PET
- Price $80 each way
- Weight limit 20 pounds
- Carrier size limit 23 in. × 13 in. × 9 in.

PET AS CARGO
- Price $100 each way
- Weight limit 100 pounds
- Carrier size limit 40 in. × 27 in. × 30 in.
- Temperature restrictions The outside temperature during the trip must be between 45° and 75° for cats and pug-nosed dogs (85° for all other dogs).

CONTINENTAL
(800) 523-3273
24 Hour Animal Desk (800) 575-3335
or (281) 553-5052
continental.com

IN-CABIN PET
- Price $95 each way
- Weight limit 10 pounds
- Carrier size limit 22 in. × 14 in. × 9 in.

PET AS CARGO
- Price $99–$329 each way
- Weight limit 150 pounds
- Carrier size limit 40 in. × 27 in. × 30 in.
- Temperature restrictions None
- Bonus Each dollar spent on pet travel is equivalent to a mile in the One Pass rewards program.

DELTA
(800) 221-1212
delta.com

IN-CABIN PET
- Price $75 each way
- Weight limit None
- Carrier size limit 17 in. × 12 in. × 8 in.

PET AS CARGO
- Price $100 each way
- Weight limit 51 pounds
- Carrier size limit 48 in. × 32 in. × 35 in.
- Temperature restrictions The outside temperature during the trip must be between 45° and 75° for cats and pug-nosed dogs (85° for all other dogs).
- Blackout days May 15–September 15

JET BLUE
(800) 538-2583
jetblue.com

IN-CABIN PET
- Price $50 each way
- Weight limit 20 pounds
- Carrier size limit 17 in. × 12.5 in. × 8 in.

PET AS CARGO
Jet Blue does not accept pets as cargo.

NORTHWEST AIRLINES
(800) 225-2525
Pet Center Information Line
(888) 692-4738
nwa.com

IN-CABIN PET
- Price $80 each way
- Weight limit 15 pounds
- Carrier size limit 17 in. × 12 in. × 8 in.

PET AS CARGO
- Price $139–$359 each way
- Weight limit 100 pounds
- Carrier size limit 40 in. × 32 in. × 35 in.
- Temperature restrictions   The outside temperature during the trip must be between 45° and 75° for cats and pug-nosed dogs (85° for all other dogs).
- Blackout days June 1–September 15

SOUTHWEST AIRLINES

Southwest permits only service animals on flights.

U.S. AIRWAYS

(800) 428-4322
usairways.com

IN-CABIN PET
- Price $80 each way
- Weight limit None
- Carrier size limit 21 in. × 16 in. × 8 in.

PET AS CARGO
- Price $100 each way. (U.S. Airways does not make reservations for pets as cargo. They operate on a first-come, first-served basis.)
- Weight limit 100 pounds
- Carrier size limit 48 in. × 32 in. × 35 in.
- Temperature restrictions   The outside temperature during the trip must be between 45° and 75° for cats and pug-nosed dogs (85° for all other dogs).

UNITED

(800) 864-8331
united.com

IN-CABIN PET
- Price $80 each way
- Weight limit 20 pounds
- Carrier size limit 17 in. × 12 in. × 8 in.

PET AS CARGO
- Price $100–$200 each way
- Weight limit 150 pounds
- Carrier size limit 40 in. × 27 in. × 30 in.
- Temperature restrictions   The outside temperature during the trip must be between 45° and 75° for cats and pug-nosed dogs (85° for all other dogs).
- Blackout days - June 1 - Sept. 15 (for specific breeds).

Notes

car rental agencies

Most car rental agencies allow pets with no additional fee or weight limit, but some insist that you keep your pet in a carrier while in the car. This is a good idea anyway since it is much safer for your cat, and you will be charged for any damage your cat does to the vehicle. To avoid a cleaning fee, make sure to clean up any pet hair before returning the car. It's always smart to confirm that the agency's policies have not changed before you travel.

AVIS
(800) 331-1212
avis.com

BUDGET
(800) 527-0700
budget.com

DOLLAR
(800) 800-3665
dollar.com

ENTERPRISE
(800) 261-7331
enterprise.com

HERTZ
(800) 654-3131
hertz.com

NATIONAL
(800) 227-7368
nationalcar.com

THRIFTY
(800) 847-4389
thrifty.com

train policies

Amtrak allows only service dogs. Local and commuter train policies vary. Call before traveling.

Notes

hotel do's and don'ts

Hotels across the nation are becoming more and more welcoming of pets. To keep pets welcome in hotels, be sure to prevent your cat from causing any damage to the hotel or disturbing any guests.

HOTEL DO'S AND DON'TS

DO Keep your cat in a carrier at all times in public spaces.

DO Put a Do Not Disturb sign on the door if you leave your cat in the room alone.

DO Make sure your cat has water at all times, especially if you've been flying — cats get dehydrated, too.

DO Bring food from home. Many hotels offer a gourmet room-service menu for pets. But unless your cat regularly dines on tuna tartare or filet mignon, the rich food may upset her stomach.

DO Bring a sheet or blanket from home to cover the hotel's bedspread and/or furniture.

DON'T Leave your cat loose in the room alone unless you are certain:

- You have the hotel's permission to do so
- Your cat won't soil, scratch, or otherwise destroy the furniture or carpet
- Your cat won't whine and disturb other guests
- Your cat won't soil outside her litter box.

Not only is the bathroom in your hotel room a good place to keep your cat's food dishes and litter box, it is also a good place to contain your cat while you are out of the room. The lack of furniture makes it difficult for your cat to cause any damage, and hard floors are much easier to clean than carpeting. If you have a particularly curious or mischievous cat, you may want to remove the towels, toilet paper, tissues, and any other toiletries she might use to amuse herself.

Be very careful every time you enter or exit the room. Even if your cat does not try to escape at home, she is in an unfamiliar environment, which may cause her to behave erratically. That said, cats are much more likely to hide than to attempt to escape. So if you think your cat has disappeared, check the following places before sending out a search party:

- Under the bed — and inside the mattress lining
- Under the covers
- Underneath or behind chairs, sofas, and other furniture — pull the furniture out far enough to check the cavities in the back (even if you are sure your cat could not possibly squeeze back there)
- In drawers or armoires
- In the closet — especially on the top shelf on or behind blankets or pillows
- Behind the TV
- Behind or inside suitcases

cat-friendly hotel chains

$	Economy	★	Basic accommodations
$$	Low cost	★ ★	Modest accommodations
$$$	Moderate	★ ★ ★	Comfortable accommodations
$$$$	Expensive	★ ★ ★ ★	Deluxe accommodations
$$$$$	Very expensive	★ ★ ★ ★ ★	Luxury accommodations

BEST WESTERN ★ ★
800) 780-7234
bestwestern.com
Price Range $$
Cat Friendly Numerous locations

CANDLEWOOD SUITES ★
(877) CANDLEWOOD
candlewoodsuites.com
Price Range $
Cat Friendly All locations (You must notify them when you make your reservation that you are bringing a pet.)

CLARION ★ ★
(877) 424-6423
clarioninn.com
Price Range $$
Cat Friendly Some Locations

COMFORT SUITES ★ ★ (COMFORT INN ★)
(877) 424-6423
choicehotels.com
Price Range $/$$
Cat Friendly Numerous locations

COURTYARD MARRIOTT ★ ★
(800) 321-2211
marriott.com
Price Range $$
Cat Friendly Some locations

CROWNE PLAZA HOTEL & RESORTS ★ ★ ★
(877) 2CROWNE
crownplaza.com
Price Range $$$
Cat Friendly Some locations

DAYS INN ★
(800) DAYSINN
daysinn.com
Price Range $
Cat Friendly Most locations

DOUBLETREE ★ ★ ★
(800) 222-8733
doubletree.hilton.com
Price Range $$$
Cat Friendly Some locations

ECONO LODGE ★
(877) 424-6423
EconoLodge.com
Price Range $
Cat Friendly Numerous locations

EMBASSY SUITES ★ ★ ★
(800) 362-2779
embassysuites.hilton.com
Price Range $$$
Cat Friendly Some locations

FAIRFIELD INN MARRIOTT ★ ★
(800) 228-2800
marriott.com/fairfieldinn/
Price Range $$
Cat Friendly Some locations

FOUR SEASONS HOTEL ★ ★ ★ ★ ★
(800) 819-5053
fourseasons.com
Price Range $$$$$
Cat Friendly Numerous (At most locations, you must get approval prior to arrival. Strict weight limits apply.)

HAMPTON INN ★ ★
(800) 426-7866
hamptoninn.hilton.com
Price Range $$
Cat Friendly Some locations

HILTON HOTELS ★ ★ ★
(800) 445-8667
hilton.com
Price Range $$$/$$$$
Cat Friendly Some locations

HOLIDAY INN ★ ★
(**HOLIDAY INN EXPRESS** ★)
(800) 315-2621
holidayinn.com/hiexpress.com
Price Range $/$$
Cat Friendly Numerous locations

HOMEWOOD SUITES BY HILTON ★
(800) 225-5466
Homewoodsuites.hilton.com
Price Range $
Cat Friendly Some locations

HOWARD JOHNSON ★
(800) 446-4656
hojo.com
Price Range $
Cat Friendly Numerous locations

INTERCONTINENTAL ★ ★ ★ ★
(800) 980-6429
intercontinental.com
Price Range $$$$
Cat Friendly Some locations

KIMPTON HOTELS ★ ★ ★ ★
(800) KIMPTON
kimptonhotels.com
Price Range $$$$
Cat Friendly Most locations

LA QUINTA INN & SUITES ★ ★ ★
(**LA QUINTA INN** ★ ★)
(866) 725-1661
lq.com
Price Range $$/$$$
Cat Friendly Most locations

LOEWS HOTELS ★ ★ ★ ★
(800) 23LOEWS
loewshotels.com
Price Range $$$$
Cat Friendly All locations

MARRIOTT ★ ★ ★
(888) 236-2427
marriott.com
Price Range $$$
Cat Friendly Some locations

MOTEL 6 ★
(800) 466-8356
motel6.com
Price Range $
Cat Friendly All locations

QUALITY INN ★ ★
(877) 424-6423
qualityinn.com
Price Range $$
Cat Friendly Numerous locations

RAMADA ★ ★
(800) 272-6232
ramada.com
Price Range $$/$$$
Cat Friendly Some locations

RED ROOF INN ★
(800) 733-7663
redroof.com
Price Range $
Cat Friendly Most locations

RENAISSANCE HOTELS AND RESORTS
MARRIOTT ★ ★ ★
(800) 468-3571
marriott.com/renaissancehotels/
Price Range $$$
Cat Friendly Some locations

RESIDENCE INN MARRIOTT ★ ★
(800) 331-3131
marriott.com/residenceinn/
Price Range $$
Cat Friendly All locations

RITZ CARLTON, THE ★ ★ ★ ★ ★
(800) 241-3333
ritzcarlton.com
Price Range $$$$$
Cat Friendly Numerous locations
(At most locations, you must get approval
prior to arrival. Strict weight limits apply.)

SHERATON HOTELS ★ ★ ★
(800) 325-3535
sheraton.com
Price Range $$$
Cat Friendly Some locations

SLEEP INN ★
(877) 424-6423
sleepinn.com
Price Range $$
Cat Friendly Some locations

SOFITEL ★ ★ ★ ★
(800) 221-4542
sofitel.com
Price Range $$$$
Cat friendly Numerous locations

ST. REGIS HOTELS & RESORTS ★ ★ ★ ★
(877) 787-3447
starwoodhotels.com/stregis/
Price Range $$$$
Cat Friendly Numerous Locations
(At most locations, you must get approval prior
to arrival. Strict weight limits apply.)

STUDIO 6 ★
(888) 897-0202
staystudio6.com
Price Range $
Cat Friendly All locations

SUPER 8 ★
(800) 800-8000
super8.com
Price Range $
Cat Friendly Numerous locations

TOWNEPLACE SUITES MARRIOTT ★ ★
(800) 257-3000
marriott.com/towneplace/
Price Range $$
Cat Friendly Some locations

TRAVELODGE ★
(800) 578-7878
travelodge.com
Price Range $
Cat Friendly Numerous locations

W HOTEL ★ ★ ★ ★
(888) 625-5144
starwoodhotels.com/whotels/
Price Range $$$$
Cat Friendly All locations

WESTIN ★ ★ ★
(800) 937-8461
starwoodhotels.com/westin/
Price Range $$$
Cat Friendly Numerous locations

WINGATE INN ★ ★
(800) 228-1000
wingateinns.com
Price Range $$
Cat Friendly Some locations

WYNDHAM HOTELS & RESORTS ★ ★ ★
(800) 996-3426
wyndham.com
Price Range $$$
Cat Friendly Numerous locations

your list of places to stay

Hotel Name . . . .

☐ Loved it
☐ Want to check it out
☐ It'll do in a bind
☐ Hated it

Address . . . .

Closest cross street . . . .

City, State, ZIP . . . .

Phone (. . . .) . . . . . . — . . . .

Web site . . . .

Deposit . . . .

Cleaning Fee . . . .

☐ Cats are not allowed in the room alone

Cat amenities . . . .

. . . .

. . . .

People amenities . . . .

. . . .

. . . .

. . . .

Nearby attractions . . . .

. . . .

. . . .

. . . .

. . . .

. . . .

Notes . . . .

. . . .

. . . .

. . . .

. . . .

your list of places to stay

Hotel Name . . . .

☐ Loved it
☐ Want to check it out
☐ It'll do in a bind
☐ Hated it

Address . . . .

Closest cross street . . . .

City, State, ZIP . . . .

Phone   (. . . .) . . . . ―

Web site . . . .

Deposit . . . .

Cleaning Fee . . . .

☐ Cats are not allowed in the room alone

Cat amenities . . . .

. . . .

. . . .

People amenities . . . .

. . . .

. . . .

. . . .

Nearby attractions . . . .

. . . .

. . . .

. . . .

. . . .

Notes . . . .

. . . .

. . . .

. . . .

. . . .

your list of places to stay

Hotel Name . . . .

☐ Loved it
☐ Want to check it out
☐ It'll do in a bind
☐ Hated it

Address . . . .

Closest cross street . . . .

City, State, ZIP . . . .

Phone   (. . . .) . . . . — . . . .

Web site . . . .

Deposit . . . .

Cleaning Fee . . . .

☐ Cats are not allowed in the room alone

Cat amenities . . . .

. . . .

. . . .

People amenities . . . .

. . . .

. . . .

. . . .

Nearby attractions . . . .

. . . .

. . . .

. . . .

. . . .

Notes . . . .

. . . .

. . . .

. . . .

. . . .

your list of places to stay

Hotel Name . . . .

☐ Loved it
☐ Want to check it out
☐ It'll do in a bind
☐ Hated it

Address . . . .

Closest cross street . . . .

City, State, ZIP . . . .

Phone (. . . .) . . . . . — . . . .

Web site . . . .

Deposit . . . .

Cleaning Fee . . . .

☐ Cats are not allowed in the room alone

Cat amenities . . . .

. . . .

. . . .

People amenities . . . .

. . . .

. . . .

. . . .

Nearby attractions . . . .

. . . .

. . . .

. . . .

. . . .

. . . .

Notes . . . .

. . . .

. . . .

. . . .

. . . .

your list of places to stay

Hotel Name . . . .

☐ Loved it
☐ Want to check it out
☐ It'll do in a bind
☐ Hated it

Address . . . .

Closest cross street . . . .

City, State, ZIP . . . .

Phone   (. . . .) . . . . . . — . . . .

Web site . . . .

Deposit . . . .

Cleaning Fee . . . .

☐ Cats are not allowed in the room alone

Cat amenities . . . .

. . . .

. . . .

People amenities . . . .

. . . .

. . . .

. . . .

Nearby attractions . . . .

. . . .

. . . .

. . . .

. . . .

. . . .

Notes . . . .

. . . .

. . . .

. . . .

. . . .

your list of places to stay

Hotel Name . . . .

☐ Loved it
☐ Want to check it out
☐ It'll do in a bind
☐ Hated it

Address . . . .

Closest cross street . . . .

City, State, ZIP . . . .

Phone   (. . . .) . . . . — . . . .

Web site . . . .

Deposit . . . .

Cleaning Fee . . . .

☐ Cats are not allowed in the room alone

Cat amenities . . . .

. . . .

. . . .

People amenities . . . .

. . . .

. . . .

. . . .

Nearby attractions . . . .

. . . .

. . . .

. . . .

. . . .

Notes . . . .

. . . .

. . . .

. . . .

. . . .

your list of places to stay

Hotel Name . . . .

☐ Loved it
☐ Want to check it out
☐ It'll do in a bind
☐ Hated it

Address . . . .

Closest cross street . . . .

City, State, ZIP . . . .

Phone (. . . .) . . . . — . . . .

Web site . . . .

Deposit . . . .

Cleaning Fee . . . .

☐ Cats are not allowed in the room alone

Cat amenities . . . .

. . . .

. . . .

People amenities . . . .

. . . .

. . . .

. . . .

Nearby attractions . . . .

. . . .

. . . .

. . . .

. . . .

. . . .

Notes . . . .

your list of places to stay

Hotel Name . . . .

☐ Loved it
☐ Want to check it out
☐ It'll do in a bind
☐ Hated it

Address . . . .

Closest cross street . . . .

City, State, ZIP . . . .

Phone   (. . . .) . . . . — . . . .

Web site . . . .

Deposit . . . .

Cleaning Fee . . . .

☐ Cats are not allowed in the room alone

Cat amenities . . . .

. . . .

. . . .

People amenities . . . .

. . . .

. . . .

. . . .

Nearby attractions . . . .

. . . .

. . . .

. . . .

. . . .

. . . .

Notes . . . .

. . . .

. . . .

. . . .

. . . .

your list of places to stay

Hotel Name . . . .

☐ Loved it
☐ Want to check it out
☐ It'll do in a bind
☐ Hated it

Address . . . .

Closest cross street . . . .

City, State, ZIP . . . .

Phone   (. . . .) . . . . ⎯ . . . .

Web site . . . .

Deposit . . . .

Cleaning Fee . . . .

☐ Cats are not allowed in the room alone

Cat amenities . . . .

. . . .

. . . .

People amenities . . . .

. . . .

. . . .

. . . .

Nearby attractions . . . .

. . . .

. . . .

. . . .

. . . .

. . . .

Notes . . . .

. . . .

. . . .

. . . .

. . . .

your list of places to stay

Hotel Name . . . .

☐ Loved it
☐ Want to check it out
☐ It'll do in a bind
☐ Hated it

Address . . . .

Closest cross street . . . .

City, State, ZIP . . . .

Phone   (. . . .) . . . . ⎯ . . . .

Web site . . . .

Deposit . . . .

Cleaning Fee . . . .

☐ Cats are not allowed in the room alone

Cat amenities . . . .

. . . .

. . . .

People amenities . . . .

. . . .

. . . .

. . . .

Nearby attractions . . . .

. . . .

. . . .

. . . .

. . . .

. . . .

Notes . . . .

. . . .

. . . .

. . . .

. . . .

Notes

Chapter 5

 LOGS & INFO SHEETS

Your cat's complete medical history is an invaluable resource to help you make cat-care choices. Use the logs to record medical events in your cat's life, and use the sheets to write down information you wish to provide to future care providers. This section will help you stay organized and consistently give the best care to your cat.

in this chapter

VACCINATION LOGS
MEDICAL/DENTAL LOGS
PET SITTER INFO SHEETS
VET INFO SHEETS

VACCINATION LOGS

CAT NAME	DATE	VACCINATION	EXPIRES

VACCINATION LOGS

CAT NAME	DATE	VACCINATION	EXPIRES

MEDICAL/DENTAL LOGS

Photocopy if you need more pages.

Cat Name . . . .   Cat Name . . . .

Date . . . .   Date . . . .

Vet/technician . . . .   Vet/technician . . . .

Reason for visit . . . .   Reason for visit . . . .

. . . .

Diagnosis . . . .   Diagnosis . . . .

. . . .

Treatment . . . .   Treatment . . . .

. . . .

Follow-up . . . .   Follow-up . . . .

. . . .

Medication . . . .   Medication . . . .

. . . .

Notes . . . .   **Notes** . . . .

. . . .

. . . .

. . . .

. . . .

MEDICAL/DENTAL LOGS

Photocopy if you need more pages.

Cat Name . . . .

Date . . . .

Vet/technician . . . .

Reason for visit . . . .

. . . .

Diagnosis . . . .

. . . .

Treatment . . . .

. . . .

Follow-up . . . .

. . . .

Medication . . . .

. . . .

. . . .

Notes . . . .

. . . .

. . . .

. . . .

. . . .

. . . .

Cat Name . . . .

Date . . . .

Vet/technician . . . .

Reason for visit . . . .

. . . .

Diagnosis . . . .

. . . .

Treatment . . . .

. . . .

Follow-up . . . .

. . . .

Medication . . . .

. . . .

. . . .

Notes . . . .

. . . .

. . . .

. . . .

. . . .

. . . .

MEDICAL/DENTAL LOGS

Photocopy if you need more pages.

Cat Name . . . .

Date . . . .

Vet/technician . . . .

Reason for visit . . . .

. . . .

Diagnosis . . . .

. . . .

Treatment . . . .

. . . .

Follow-up . . . .

. . . .

Medication . . . .

. . . .

. . . .

Notes . . . .

. . . .

. . . .

. . . .

. . . .

. . . .

Cat Name . . . .

Date . . . .

Vet/technician . . . .

Reason for visit . . . .

. . . .

Diagnosis . . . .

. . . .

Treatment . . . .

. . . .

Follow-up . . . .

. . . .

Medication . . . .

. . . .

. . . .

Notes . . . .

. . . .

. . . .

. . . .

. . . .

. . . .

MEDICAL/DENTAL LOGS

Photocopy if you need more pages.

Cat Name . . . .

Date . . . .

Vet/technician . . . .

Reason for visit . . . .

. . . .

Diagnosis . . . .

. . . .

Treatment . . . .

. . . .

Follow-up . . . .

. . . .

Medication . . . .

. . . .

. . . .

Notes . . . .

. . . .

. . . .

. . . .

. . . .

. . . .

Cat Name . . . .

Date . . . .

Vet/technician . . . .

Reason for visit . . . .

. . . .

Diagnosis . . . .

. . . .

Treatment . . . .

. . . .

Follow-up . . . .

. . . .

Medication . . . .

. . . .

. . . .

Notes . . . .

. . . .

. . . .

. . . .

. . . .

. . . .

MEDICAL/DENTAL LOGS

Photocopy if you need more pages.

Cat Name . . . .

Date . . . .

Vet/technician . . . .

Reason for visit . . . .

. . . .

Diagnosis . . . .

. . . .

Treatment . . . .

. . . .

Follow-up . . . .

. . . .

Medication . . . .

. . . .

. . . .

Notes . . . .

. . . .

. . . .

. . . .

. . . .

Cat Name . . . .

Date . . . .

Vet/technician . . . .

Reason for visit . . . .

. . . .

Diagnosis . . . .

. . . .

Treatment . . . .

. . . .

Follow-up . . . .

. . . .

Medication . . . .

. . . .

. . . .

Notes . . . .

. . . .

. . . .

. . . .

. . . .

MEDICAL/DENTAL LOGS

Photocopy if you need more pages.

Cat Name . . . .

Date . . . .

Vet/technician . . . .

Reason for visit . . . .

. . . .

Diagnosis . . . .

. . . .

Treatment . . . .

. . . .

Follow-up . . . .

. . . .

Medication . . . .

. . . .

. . . .

Cat Name . . . .

Date . . . .

Vet/technician . . . .

Reason for visit . . . .

. . . .

Diagnosis . . . .

. . . .

Treatment . . . .

. . . .

Follow-up . . . .

. . . .

Medication . . . .

. . . .

. . . .

Notes . . . .

. . . .

. . . .

. . . .

. . . .

. . . .

Notes . . . .

. . . .

. . . .

. . . .

. . . .

. . . .

Notes

PET SITTER INFO SHEETS

Cut out these handy sheets (or bookmark with a stickie) for pet sitters.

cat name . . . .

CAT OWNER 1

Name . . . .

Phone (. . . .) . . . . . — . . . . .

Cell phone (. . . .) . . . . . — . . . . .

Work phone (. . . .) . . . . . — . . . . .

Destination (. . . .) . . . . . — . . . . .

VET

Name . . . .

Phone (. . . .) . . . . . — . . . . .

Address . . . .

Closest cross street . . . .

City, State, ZIP . . . .

EMERGENCY CONTACT

Name . . . .

Phone (. . . .) . . . . . — . . . . .

Cell phone (. . . .) . . . . . — . . . . .

CAT OWNER 2

Name . . . .

Phone (. . . .) . . . . . — . . . . .

Cell phone (. . . .) . . . . . — . . . . .

Work phone (. . . .) . . . . . — . . . . .

Destination (. . . .) . . . . . — . . . . .

EMERGENCY FACILITY

Name . . . .

Phone (. . . .) . . . . . — . . . . .

Address . . . .

Closest cross street . . . .

City, State, ZIP . . . .

I have allergies ☐ Yes ☐ No

My allergies are . . . .

. . . .

If I have an allergic reaction . . . .

. . . .

I am on medication ☐ Yes ☐ No

Medication . . . .

Dosage/frequency . . . .

Give with . . . .

Medication . . . .

Dosage/frequency . . . .

Give with . . . .

eating

I eat. . . . . cup(s)/can(s) of. . . . .

. . . .

Special preparation . . . .

. . . .

My food is kept . . . .

. . . .

☐ I eat breakfast at . . . .

☐ I eat dinner at . . . .

☐ I eat once a day at . . . .

☐ I do **not** like to be touched while eating

My treats are kept . . . .

☐ I am allowed to have . . . . treats a day

☐ No treats for me — I am
    ☐ on a diet
    ☐ allergic

I ☐ **am** ☐ **am not** allowed to eat table scraps

  ☐ Except ☐ Only . . . .

attitude

I may have an issue with
    ☐ Other cats
    ☐ Small dogs
    ☐ Big dogs
    ☐ All dogs
    ☐ Visitors
    ☐ Children
    ☐ Separation anxiety
    ☐ Other. . . . .

Given the opportunity, I will...

    ☐ Curl up in your lap and go to sleep
    ☐ Scratch your eyes out
    ☐ Rub against you and look for rubs
    ☐ Scratch my scratching post
    ☐ Escape
    ☐ Other . . . .

Notes . . . .

. . . .

. . . .

. . . .

. . . .

. . . .

PET SITTER INFO SHEETS

Cut out these handy sheets (or bookmark with a stickie) for pet sitters.

cat name . . . .

CAT OWNER 1

Name . . . .

Phone (. . . .) . . . . . . — . . . .

Cell phone (. . . .) . . . . . . — . . . .

Work phone (. . . .) . . . . . — . . . .

Destination (. . . .) . . . . . — . . . . . .

VET

Name . . . .

Phone (. . . .) . . . . . — . . . .

Address . . . .

Closest cross street . . . .

City, State, ZIP . . . .

EMERGENCY CONTACT

Name . . . .

Phone (. . . .) . . . . . — . . . .

Cell phone (. . . .) . . . . . — . . . .

I am on medication ☐ Yes ☐ No

Medication . . . .

Dosage/frequency . . . .

Give with . . . .

CAT OWNER 2

Name . . . .

Phone (. . . .) . . . . . . — . . . .

Cell phone (. . . .) . . . . . . — . . . .

Work phone (. . . .) . . . . . — . . . .

Destination (. . . .) . . . . . — . . . . . .

EMERGENCY FACILITY

Name . . . .

Phone (. . . .) . . . . . — . . . .

Address . . . .

Closest cross street . . . .

City, State, ZIP . . . .

I have allergies ☐ Yes ☐ No

My allergies are . . . .

. . . .

If I have an allergic reaction . . . .

. . . .

Medication . . . .

Dosage/frequency . . . .

Give with . . . .

eating

I eat. . . . . cup(s)/can(s) of. . . . .

. . . .

Special preparation . . . .

. . . .

My food is kept . . . .

. . . .

☐ I eat breakfast at . . . .

☐ I eat dinner at . . . .

☐ I eat once a day at . . . .

☐ I do **not** like to be touched while eating

My treats are kept . . . .

☐ I am allowed to have . . . . treats a day

☐ No treats for me — I am
    ☐ on a diet
    ☐ allergic

I ☐ **am** ☐ **am not** allowed to eat table scraps

☐ Except ☐ Only . . . .

attitude

I may have an issue with
    ☐ Other cats
    ☐ Small dogs
    ☐ Big dogs
    ☐ All dogs
    ☐ Visitors
    ☐ Children
    ☐ Separation anxiety
    ☐ Other. . . . .

Given the opportunity, I will...

☐ Curl up in your lap and go to sleep
☐ Scratch your eyes out
☐ Rub against you and look for rubs
☐ Scratch my scratching post
☐ Escape
☐ Other . . . .

Notes . . . .

. . . .

. . . .

. . . .

. . . .

. . . .

PET SITTER INFO SHEETS

Cut out these handy sheets (or bookmark with a stickie) for pet sitters.

cat name . . . .

CAT OWNER 1

Name . . . .

Phone (. . . .) . . . . . . — . . . . .

Cell phone (. . . .) . . . . . . — . . . . .

Work phone (. . . .) . . . . . . — . . . . .

Destination (. . . .) . . . . . . — . . . . .

VET

Name . . . .

Phone (. . . .) . . . . . . — . . . . .

Address . . . .

Closest cross street . . . .

City, State, ZIP . . . .

EMERGENCY CONTACT

Name . . . .

Phone (. . . .) . . . . . . — . . . . .

Cell phone (. . . .) . . . . . . — . . . . .

I am on medication ☐ Yes ☐ No

Medication . . . .

Dosage/frequency . . . .

Give with . . . .

CAT OWNER 2

Name . . . .

Phone (. . . .) . . . . . . — . . . . .

Cell phone (. . . .) . . . . . . — . . . . .

Work phone (. . . .) . . . . . . — . . . . .

Destination (. . . .) . . . . . . — . . . . .

EMERGENCY FACILITY

Name . . . .

Phone (. . . .) . . . . . . — . . . . .

Address . . . .

Closest cross street . . . .

City, State, ZIP . . . .

I have allergies ☐ Yes ☐ No

My allergies are . . . .

. . . .

If I have an allergic reaction . . . .

. . . .

Medication . . . .

Dosage/frequency . . . .

Give with . . . .

eating

I eat. . . . . cup(s)/can(s) of . . . .

. . . .

Special preparation . . . .

. . . .

My food is kept . . . .

. . . .

☐ I eat breakfast at . . . .

☐ I eat dinner at . . . .

☐ I eat once a day at . . . .

☐ I do **not** like to be touched while eating

My treats are kept . . . .

☐ I am allowed to have . . . . . . treats a day

☐ No treats for me — I am
    ☐ on a diet
    ☐ allergic

I ☐ **am** ☐ **am not** allowed to eat table scraps

☐ Except ☐ Only . . . .

attitude

I may have an issue with
    ☐ Other cats
    ☐ Small dogs
    ☐ Big dogs
    ☐ All dogs
    ☐ Visitors
    ☐ Children
    ☐ Separation anxiety
    ☐ Other. . . . .

Given the opportunity, I will...

☐ Curl up in your lap and go to sleep
☐ Scratch your eyes out
☐ Rub against you and look for rubs
☐ Scratch my scratching post
☐ Escape
☐ Other . . . .

Notes . . . .

. . . .

. . . .

. . . .

. . . .

. . . .

PET SITTER INFO SHEETS

Cut out these handy sheets (or bookmark with a stickie) for pet sitters.

cat name . . . .

CAT OWNER 1

Name . . . .

Phone (. . . .) . . . . — . . . .

Cell phone (. . . .) . . . . — . . . .

Work phone (. . . .) . . . . — . . . .

Destination (. . . .) . . . . — . . . .

VET

Name . . . .

Phone (. . . .) . . . . — . . . .

Address . . . .

Closest cross street . . . .

City, State, ZIP . . . .

EMERGENCY CONTACT

Name . . . .

Phone (. . . .) . . . . — . . . .

Cell phone (. . . .) . . . . — . . . .

CAT OWNER 2

Name . . . .

Phone (. . . .) . . . . — . . . .

Cell phone (. . . .) . . . . — . . . .

Work phone (. . . .) . . . . — . . . .

Destination (. . . .) . . . . — . . . .

EMERGENCY FACILITY

Name . . . .

Phone (. . . .) . . . . — . . . .

Address . . . .

Closest cross street . . . .

City, State, ZIP . . . .

I have allergies ☐ Yes ☐ No

My allergies are . . . .

. . . .

If I have an allergic reaction . . . .

. . . .

I am on medication ☐ Yes ☐ No

Medication . . . .

Dosage/frequency . . . .

Give with . . . .

Medication . . . .

Dosage/frequency . . . .

Give with . . . .

eating

I eat . . . . . cup(s)/can(s) of . . . .

. . . .

Special preparation . . . .

. . . .

My food is kept . . . .

. . . .

☐ I eat breakfast at . . . .

☐ I eat dinner at . . . .

☐ I eat once a day at . . . .

☐ I do **not** like to be touched while eating

My treats are kept . . . .

☐ I am allowed to have . . . . treats a day

☐ No treats for me — I am
    ☐ on a diet
    ☐ allergic

I ☐ **am** ☐ **am not** allowed to eat table scraps

  ☐ Except ☐ Only . . . .

attitude

I may have an issue with
  ☐ Other cats
  ☐ Small dogs
  ☐ Big dogs
  ☐ All dogs
  ☐ Visitors
  ☐ Children
  ☐ Separation anxiety
  ☐ Other . . . .

Given the opportunity, I will...

  ☐ Curl up in your lap and go to sleep
  ☐ Scratch your eyes out
  ☐ Rub against you and look for rubs
  ☐ Scratch my scratching post
  ☐ Escape
  ☐ Other . . . .

Notes . . . .

. . . .

. . . .

. . . .

. . . .

. . . .

VET INFO SHEETS

Cut out these handy sheets to take with you to your veterinarian.

cat name . . . .

CAT OWNER 1   CAT OWNER 2

Name . . . .   Name . . . .

Home phone (. . . .) . . . . ― . .   Home phone (. . . .) . . . . . . ― . . .

Cell phone (. . . .) . . . . . ― . . .   Cell phone (. . . .) . . . . . ― . . .

Work phone (. . . .) . . . . . ― . . .   Work phone (. . . .) . . . . . ― . . .

PLEASE DON'T FORGET THAT I... (BITE, AM ALLERGIC TO, ETC.) . . . .

. . . .

MY SYMPTOMS INCLUDE

Intermittent/constant . . . . for the last . . . hours/days/weeks/months

Intermittent/constant . . . . for the last . . . hours/days/weeks/months

Intermittent/constant . . . . for the last . . . hours/days/weeks/months

Intermittent/constant . . . . for the last . . . hours/days/weeks/months

Intermittent/constant . . . . for the last . . . hours/days/weeks/months

REASONS WHY I MIGHT BE FEELING UNDER THE WEATHER

. . . .

. . . .

. . . .

. . . .

I ☐ **have** ☐ **have not** been eating regularly

I ☐ **have** ☐ **have not** been eliminating regularly

I ☐ **have** ☐ **have not** been sleeping regularly

I ☐ **have** ☐ **have not** been playing regularly

Since I am here anyway, would you also please check

....

....

....

....

Notes ....

....

....

....

....

....

....

....

....

....

....

....

VET INFO SHEETS

Cut out these handy sheets to take with you to your veterinarian.

cat name ....

CAT OWNER 1

Name . . . .

Home phone (. . . .) . . . . . . — . . . .

Cell phone (. . . .) . . . . . . — . . . .

Work phone (. . . .) . . . . . . — . . . .

CAT OWNER 2

Name . . . .

Home phone (. . . .) . . . . . . — . . . .

Cell phone (. . . .) . . . . . . — . . . .

Work phone (. . . .) . . . . . . — . . . .

PLEASE DON'T FORGET THAT I... (BITE, AM ALLERGIC TO, ETC.) . . . .

. . . .

MY SYMPTOMS INCLUDE

Intermittent/constant . . . . for the last . . . hours/days/weeks/months

Intermittent/constant . . . . for the last . . . hours/days/weeks/months

Intermittent/constant . . . . for the last . . . hours/days/weeks/months

Intermittent/constant . . . . for the last . . . hours/days/weeks/months

Intermittent/constant . . . . for the last . . . hours/days/weeks/months

REASONS WHY I MIGHT BE FEELING UNDER THE WEATHER

. . . .

. . . .

. . . .

. . . .

I ☐ **have** ☐ **have not** been eating regularly

I ☐ **have** ☐ **have not** been eliminating regularly

I ☐ **have** ☐ **have not** been sleeping regularly

I ☐ **have** ☐ **have not** been playing regularly

Since I am here anyway, would you also please check

. . . .

. . . .

. . . .

. . . .

Notes . . . .

. . . .

. . . .

. . . .

. . . .

. . . .

. . . .

. . . .

. . . .

. . . .

. . . .

VET INFO SHEETS

Cut out these handy sheets to take with you to your veterinarian.

cat name . . . .

CAT OWNER 1

Name . . . .

Home phone (. . . .) . . . . — . . . .

Cell phone (. . . .) . . . . . . — . . . .

Work phone (. . . .) . . . . . . — . . . . . .

CAT OWNER 2

Name . . . .

Home phone (. . . .) . . . . . . — . . . .

Cell phone (. . . .) . . . . . . — . . . .

Work phone (. . . .) . . . . . . — . . . .

PLEASE DON'T FORGET THAT I... (BITE, AM ALLERGIC TO, ETC.) . . . .

. . . .

MY SYMPTOMS INCLUDE

Intermittent/constant . . . . for the last . . . . hours/days/weeks/months

Intermittent/constant . . . . for the last . . . . hours/days/weeks/months

Intermittent/constant . . . . for the last . . . . hours/days/weeks/months

Intermittent/constant . . . . for the last . . . . hours/days/weeks/months

Intermittent/constant . . . . for the last . . . . hours/days/weeks/months

REASONS WHY I MIGHT BE FEELING UNDER THE WEATHER

. . . .

. . . .

. . . .

. . . .

I ☐ **have** ☐ **have not** been eating regularly

I ☐ **have** ☐ **have not** been eliminating regularly

I ☐ **have** ☐ **have not** been sleeping regularly

I ☐ **have** ☐ **have not** been playing regularly

Since I am here anyway, would you also please check

. . . .

. . . .

. . . .

. . . .

Notes . . . .

. . . .

. . . .

. . . .

. . . .

. . . .

. . . .

. . . .

. . . .

. . . .

. . . .

. . . .

VET INFO SHEETS

Cut out these handy sheets to take with you to your veterinarian.

cat name ....

CAT OWNER 1

Name . . . .

Home phone (. . . .) . . . . . . — . . . . . .

Cell phone (. . . .) . . . . . . — . . . . . .

Work phone (. . . .) . . . . . . — . . . . . .

CAT OWNER 2

Name . . . .

Home phone (. . . .) . . . . . . — . . . . . .

Cell phone (. . . .) . . . . . . — . . . . . .

Work phone (. . . .) . . . . . . — . . . . . .

PLEASE DON'T FORGET THAT I... (BITE, AM ALLERGIC TO, ETC.) . . . .

. . . .

MY SYMPTOMS INCLUDE

Intermittent/constant . . . . for the last . . . hours/days/weeks/months

Intermittent/constant . . . . for the last . . . hours/days/weeks/months

Intermittent/constant . . . . for the last . . . hours/days/weeks/months

Intermittent/constant . . . . for the last . . . hours/days/weeks/months

Intermittent/constant . . . . for the last . . . hours/days/weeks/months

REASONS WHY I MIGHT BE FEELING UNDER THE WEATHER

. . . .

. . . .

. . . .

. . . .

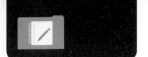

I ☐ **have** ☐ **have not** been eating regularly

I ☐ **have** ☐ **have not** been eliminating regularly

I ☐ **have** ☐ **have not** been sleeping regularly

I ☐ **have** ☐ **have not** been playing regularly

Since I am here anyway, would you also please check

. . . .

. . . .

. . . .

. . . .

Notes . . . .

. . . .

. . . .

. . . .

. . . .

. . . .

. . . .

. . . .

. . . .

. . . .

. . . .

. . . .